THE
SIX WIVES
OF
HENRY VIII

ADVENTURES IN TIME
BY
DOMINIC SANDBROOK

PUBLISHED

The Second World War
The Six Wives of Henry VIII

FORTHCOMING

Alexander the Great
The First World War
Cleopatra
The Vikings
The Conquest of the Americas
Napoleon

ADVENTURES IN TIME
BY
DOMINIC SANDBROOK

THE
SIX WIVES
OF
HENRY VIII

with illustrations by Edward Bettison

PARTICULAR BOOKS
an imprint of
PENGUIN BOOKS

PARTICULAR BOOKS

UK | USA | Canada | Ireland | Australia
India | New Zealand | South Africa

Particular Books is part of the Penguin Random House group of companies
whose addresses can be found at global.penguinrandomhouse.com

First published in Particular Books 2021

002

Text copyright © Dominic Sandbrook 2021

Illustrations and maps © Edward Bettison, 2021

The moral rights of the author have been asserted

Set in 12.51/16.58pt Bembo Book MT Std
Typeset by Jouve (UK), Milton Keynes
Printed and bound in Great Britain by Clays Ltd, Elcograf S.p.A.

The authorized representative in the EEA is Penguin Random House Ireland,
Morrison Chambers, 32 Nassau Street, Dublin D02 YH68

A CIP catalogue record for this book is available from the British Library

ISBN: 978–0–241–46973–6

www.greenpenguin.co.uk

MIX
Paper from
responsible sources
FSC® C018179

Penguin Random House is committed to a
sustainable future for our business, our readers
and our planet. This book is made from Forest
Stewardship Council® certified paper.

For Tamsin and Juliana Jenkinson

Contents

CONTENTS

The Battle

Dawn broke early over the heart of England. On the ridge, campfires burned in the grey half-light.

Already King Richard's officers were awake, rousing their men to pull on their armour. The jangle of harnesses, the twang of bowstrings, the ring of hammers drifted through the morning air.

Above the King's tent the flags of England and St George fluttered alongside his personal banner, the fierce-tusked white boar. As his captains gathered for their final instructions, Richard Plantagenet stood framed in the entrance. A servant held his helmet, with its glittering golden crown.

Richard III had been king for barely two years. He was a ruthless, unsparing man. For almost all his life, England had been at war, torn apart by the great families' lust for the throne.

Men said Richard had murdered his little nephews to get his hands on the crown. The two boys had vanished from the Tower of London, never to be seen again.

But Richard knew a king could have no room in his

heart for pity. Victory went to the man who took risks, who moved first and was not afraid to shed blood.

Now, after the long years of war, almost all his rivals were dead. There was just one contender left, a young Welsh adventurer with a rag-tag army.

For the last few days, Richard had pursued his prey across England. And by the morning of 22 August 1485, near the village of Bosworth, Leicestershire, he had found him.

Now Richard stared down at the rebels below, his eyes clear and cold.

In just a few hours, he told his captains, they would be celebrating their crowning victory. Their enemy was a 'Welsh milksop' leading a gang of 'traitors, thieves, outlaws and renegades'.

Now Richard raised his voice. 'This day I will triumph by glorious victory,' he cried, 'or suffer death for immortal fame!'

A great roar rose from the royal army. Their swords gleamed in the morning sun. This was it: the last battle.

On the plain below, the rebels, too, were moving. Few of them had managed to get much sleep.

Beneath his Red Dragon banner, a slender young man with sharp, thoughtful eyes gazed up at the royal army. Born in Wales, Henry Tudor had spent most of his life on the run.

His father had been killed before he was born. Sheltered by his uncle, he had spent years hiding across the sea, in France and Brittany.

Two weeks earlier Henry had landed in Wales with a little band of sea-soaked followers, hoping to gather support as he went along. But few men had rallied to his banners. By the time he reached Bosworth, his ranks had grown to just five thousand, barely half of the size of King Richard's army.

Henry had always been a cautious, careful man. Now, as he pulled on his armour, he knew his future had come down to this last despairing stand.

For days he had been sending messages to the most powerful noble family in England, the Stanleys, begging for support. Across the fields he could make out their soldiers' battle-red surcoats in the dawn half-light.

But the Stanleys had made no move to join the rebels. Deep down, Henry knew they were waiting to see which side proved the stronger.

As his captains gathered around him, he searched for the right words. 'Remember,' he said, 'that victory is not won with the multitudes of men, but with the courage of hearts and the valiantness of minds.

'Let us therefore fight like invincible giants, and banish all fears like ramping lions. And now advance forward, true men against traitors, true inheritors against usurpers, the scourges of God against tyrants!'

Cheers rang through the rebel ranks. But as Henry lowered his visor, he could feel the fear building inside him.

All his life he had been the plaything of fate. But now, when it mattered most, it seemed his luck had run out.

Cannon fire thundered around the field of Bosworth. King Richard's foot soldiers were streaming downhill, their voices raised in bloodcurdling battle-cries.

Halfway down the hill, the two lines met in a clash of steel. Everywhere men were falling, shouting, screaming, dying.

Henry Tudor's men were fighting valiantly, but they were badly outnumbered. They had not yet been broken, but it was surely only a matter of time.

In mounting desperation, Henry looked across the fields to the red ranks of the Stanleys. Still their men stood and waited.

Now he saw movement on the crest of the slope, a flash of silver in the morning sun. Richard's knights were charging, their red banners streaming in the breeze, the air ringing with their triumphant war-songs.

Frozen in horror, Henry watched them sweep around the main battle. Moments later, galloping at full speed, they were on him.

With a sickening, splintering crash, the knights slammed into Henry's little group. And at their head was a figure in gleaming armour, his blood-stained battle-axe rising and falling, his helmet encircled with glinting gold.

It was Richard. Onwards he came, unstoppable, invincible, his eyes glittering with the joy of slaughter.

Henry's head was spinning, his horse rearing in fear. The Red Dragon banner was down, trampled underfoot. Richard was barely a spear's length away now.

And suddenly, in the distance, as if from another world, Henry heard voices crying in surprise and anger. He turned his head, and saw an oncoming storm of men in scarlet, a tide sweeping Richard's knights to their deaths.

With an unutterable surge of relief and joy, Henry knew he was saved. The Stanleys had come at last.

Richard, too, had turned to face the newcomers. He was laying about him with his axe, raging furiously against the turn of fortune, his hoarse voice screaming: 'Treason! Treason!'

But there were too many of them now, pushing him back, hemming him in. His horse lost its footing. Blows rained down.

The last Plantagenet was on the ground, fighting to get up. His helmet had come loose. Swords and halberds were coming at him out of the sky.

Then thunder crashed inside Richard's head, and there was only darkness.*

A few minutes later, Henry, too, was on his knees, his face streaked with sweat and mud, his eyes closed in prayer. The sound of battle was fading now. It was over.

He raised his head, and looked up. Lord Stanley was coming towards him, with something in his hand.

One of his men had found it in a hawthorn bush, he said. It must have rolled loose when the tyrant's helmet had come off.

The crown looked so thin, so delicate, its pale gold gleaming in the noonday sun. This was what it had all been for.

Reverently, almost gently, Lord Stanley placed the golden circlet on the new King's head. And as Henry VII, first of the Tudors, rose to his feet, the cheers echoed across the fields of England.

---

* Lost for centuries, Richard's body was found in 2012 beneath a Leicester car park. It was probably not the fate he would have wanted.

In the last years of the fifteenth century, every man and woman in the land knew the story of the wheel of fortune. One moment you were at the top, enjoying wealth, fame and good luck. But before you knew it, fate had turned the wheel again, sending you plunging into disgrace and despair.

'And thus does Fortune's wheel turn treacherously,' wrote the poet Geoffrey Chaucer in his book *The Canterbury Tales*, 'and out of happiness bring men to sorrow.'

Rarely, though, had the wheel turned as dramatically as it did at Bosworth. In a few hours, on a field in Leicestershire, England's history had changed for ever.

With Henry's victory, the long years of civil war were over. A new age – the age of the Tudors – had begun.

But even as the crown gleamed on Henry VII's brow, the wheel continued to turn. And this book tells the story of what happened next.

It is the story of Henry's son: the second Tudor king, Henry VIII, and of the six women who married him.

This younger Henry was one of the most magnetic characters in English history. Tall, handsome, charming and clever, a fine musician and a magnificent sportsman, he was also grasping, impulsive, suspicious and cruel.

He began his reign as the dashing image of knightly chivalry. He ended it as a bloated, stinking whale, hated and feared across the land.

But in his determination to honour his father's victory and preserve the Tudor dynasty, Henry VIII changed England in ways that still echo today.

Around him he gathered a host of colourful personalities.

There was Cardinal Wolsey, greedy, ambitious and formidably clever, the butcher's son who became a red-robed mastermind.

There was Thomas More, the ashen-faced fanatic who burned his enemies at the stake, but who was revered across Europe for choosing to risk death himself rather than betray his principles.

And there was Thomas Cromwell, the grand master of secrets and spies, determined to transform England for ever by breaking the grip of the Roman Catholic Church.

One by one, these men soared to spectacular peaks of wealth and power. But then the wheel of fortune turned, and the sword of Nemesis came swooping down.

Above all, though, this is the story of the six women who became Henry's wives.

Catherine of Aragon – the Spanish princess who found herself trapped and betrayed, far from home, but summoned the courage to fight on to the end.

Anne Boleyn – witty and edgy, clever and cruel, the diplomat's daughter who stole a king's heart but saw her dreams of glory collapse in treachery and horror.

Jane Seymour – gentle, modest and kind, the fair young woman who bore Henry the son he wanted but whose story ended in terrible tragedy.

Anne of Cleves – the frightened girl from a German castle, cruelly humiliated and cast aside, who turned herself into the great survivor of the Tudor court.

Catherine Howard – the pretty, giggly teenager who

loved music and dancing, boys and parties, but was dragged to her death in heart-rending terror.

Catherine Parr – thoughtful, brave and shrewd, the nobleman's widow who discovered a plot to overthrow her and lived to tell the tale.

These were the six wives of Henry VIII, whose stories changed England for ever.

In their different ways, they were all extraordinary women. All six have their admirers, and people still love to debate their relative merits today.

Enough. On with the story.

The scene changes; the sunlight fades. Four months have passed, and the battlefield of Bosworth is behind us now.

Winter has come, and in a far distant land, a warrior queen is expecting a child.

So begins the tale of Catherine of Aragon, the girl from Castile.

PALACES, HOUSES
1. The More, Hertfordshire
2. Hatfield, Hertfordshire
3. Buckden, Huntingdonshire
4. Kimbolton, Huntingdonshire
5. Wolf Hall, Wiltshire
6. Syon, Isleworth

Part of Scotland

York

Doncaster

Louth

Lincoln

Leicester

Walsingham

Ludlow

Wales

Ipswich

④ ③

② ①

Richmond ⑥

London

Esher

Rochester

⑤ Dogmersfield

Canterbury

Exeter

Portsmouth

Plymouth

The Kingdom of
ENGLAND

PART ONE

CATHERINE OF ARAGON

I

The Girl from Castile

On the dusty plain of the Kingdom of Castile, in the centre of what is now Spain, stands the town of Alcalá de Henares.

It is a town of narrow, cobbled streets and leafy, shaded squares, of splendid stone palaces and soaring church towers. In the summer, when its pale stone bakes beneath the blazing sun, Alcalá's squares are full of people, laughing and gossiping in the shaded cafes.

But this story begins in winter, four months after the Battle of Bosworth.

It was a grey, chilly day. The weak sun struggled to break through the clouds. For weeks the rain had hammered down, turning the roads to mud. As the wind whipped in from the plain, the townsfolk hurried along the winding alleys, too cold to linger long.

But in the town's most splendid building, the Archbishop's Palace, all was excitement. Queen Isabella was expecting a child. And on 16 December 1485, the courtiers waiting outside the royal apartment heard the high, shrill cry of a newborn infant.

The news spread quickly. God had given Isabella a little girl. It had not been easy; but the Lord be praised, both mother and daughter were well.

Soon the streets of Alcalá were alive with celebrations. With Christmas only nine days away, it was party season anyway, but now the lords and ladies of Castile had another reason to dance and sing.

As for the little girl, she was healthy and strong, with perfect white skin and the first wisps of red-blonde hair. Her mother called her Catalina, after her own grandmother. But history remembers her as Catherine of Aragon.

From the moment she emerged bawling into the world, Catherine had an exceptional destiny. She was not just any little girl. She was the daughter of Ferdinand, King of Aragon, and Isabella, Queen of Castile, the most celebrated couple in all Europe.

Married when they were teenagers, Catherine's parents had long dreamed of uniting their separate kingdoms into a single mighty realm of Spain. Year after year they had spent their summers on horseback, leading their armies across the wide southern plains, their swords glittering in the blazing sunlight.

Ferdinand was famously cunning, but Isabella was a truly extraordinary character. At a time when few women were allowed to wield power, she was determined to rule Castile herself, rallying her troops against their age-old enemies, the Moors of the south.

With her mother always on the move, little Catherine

had to get used to life on campaign. Every few days they stayed in a different castle. There was always some new monastery to visit, some new battle to fight. In her first sixteen years, Catherine and her mother celebrated Christmas in thirteen different cities.

Danger was never far away. When Catherine was young, a fire broke out in her mother's camp, and on another occasion Moorish raiders came perilously close to catching them.

Yet, despite her royal blood and adventurous childhood, Catherine was a girl like any other. As a toddler she had a little pushcart to help her walk, and she adored fruit jellies and a sugary drink known as 'rose honey'.

Since she was a princess, she was never short of presents. When she was five, she was given material to make dolls' clothes. When she was six, she was given her first jewellery, a gold headband and some bracelets. And by the time she was nine, she had a chess set and her first high heels – a pair of shoes known as chopines, to keep her feet out of the mud.

Girls did not go to school in those days. But Queen Isabella hired private tutors from Italy, who accompanied the royal family on campaign. Under their supervision, Catherine learned to read and write, not just in Spanish but in Latin, the ancient tongue of the Romans which was still the language of learning and government.

She learned to sing and to draw, to sew shirts and ride horses. She studied heraldry, learning the stories behind noble families' symbols and badges. She even studied the law, for as a princess she would need to know the rules under which countries were governed.

Every day, Catherine studied the Bible. Her mother took her faith extremely seriously, and expected her daughter to know the teachings of Jesus, the lives of the saints and the history of the early Christians.

But there was time for fun, too. Catherine and her older sister Maria loved to play chess and cards, board games and word games. They had dancing lessons with teachers from neighbouring Portugal.

Perhaps above all, they loved stories of knights and princesses, adventure and chivalry. They enjoyed hearing about the greatest of all Castilian knights, El Cid, who had fought for both the Moors and the Christians.

Of all the books in her mother's library, though, one story above all stood out: the legend of Arthur, the boy who pulled the sword from the stone to become the Once and Future King of Britain.

To children like young Catherine, this was the most inspiring tale of all. In every palace in Europe, minstrels sang of the dashing Knights of the Round Table, the mysterious Merlin, the treacherous Mordred, the handsome Lancelot and the tragic Guinevere – characters whose fame would last for ever.

In the story of Arthur and his doomed court, all human life was there: birth and death, blood and beauty, courage and cruelty, loyalty and betrayal. And running like a scarlet thread through it all was love – a passion inspiring songs and battles, invincible devotion and undying hatred.

Catherine would not have been human if she had not pictured herself as one of the lovelorn ladies at Arthur's court. But never, not in her wildest dreams, did she imagine how her own love story would turn out.

Nine days before Christmas 1498, Catherine turned thirteen. She was no longer a girl now; she was poised to become a young woman.

Whenever she looked in a mirror, a fashionably pale, oval face gazed back at her. Her eyes were blue and clear; her fair hair fell long and thick, glinting red-gold in the Spanish sun.

She was short and stocky, and nobody ever described her as a great beauty. But there was a likeable calm and seriousness about her, a sense of grace and gravity.

By now, her wanderings were almost at an end. A few months later, as the summer heat began to build, Catherine rode south across the plains of Castile, towards the distant southern mountains.

Her destination was the most celebrated of all Spain's great palaces: the dazzling jewel of the Alhambra, in the city of Granada.

Nestling beneath the snow-capped peaks of the Sierra

Nevada, Granada was a rich melting pot of mosques, churches and synagogues, where Muslims, Christians and Jews worshipped side by side.

For centuries it had been the capital of the Moorish Emirs, the last of the great Muslim dynasties who ruled the sweltering south. But gradually the Christian kings had fought their way into the mountains, driving their enemies back.

The end had come at the beginning of 1492, when Catherine was just six years old. After a gruelling siege, the last Emir of Granada surrendered the keys to Ferdinand and Isabella and rode sadly out of the city.

According to legend, the Emir stopped on a mountain peak, looked back at his beloved city, and wept. 'You cry like a woman,' his aged mother said scornfully, 'for what you could not defend like a man.'

Catherine rode into the city on the second day of July 1499, in the heat and dust of midsummer. From the slender towers of the city's mosques, the Muslim call to prayer echoed through the streets. But Catherine's destination was the walled citadel overlooking the city – the Alhambra.

Built more than a century earlier, the Alhambra was already shrouded in legend. On its high, rocky outcrop, behind its honey-coloured walls, the Moors had built a paradise of marble courtyards and painted ceilings, crystal-perfect pools and gently bubbling fountains, lush lemon trees and fragrant orange blossom.

Here at last, Catherine and her parents made their

home. And for a thirteen-year-old girl, wandering in the gardens as the prayer-calls drifted across the city below, the Alhambra seemed like a fairy tale.

Yet, all the time, Catherine knew that this was just a short-lived dream of beauty, from which she would soon awake.

As a princess, her destiny had been laid down from the moment she was born. It was her duty to make a marriage that would strengthen the glory of Spain, no matter where that path would take her.

Even as their daughter was learning to walk, Ferdinand and Isabella had been planning her future. And as they gazed at the map of Europe, there seemed an obvious candidate.

A thousand miles to the north, Henry Tudor's kingdom was a natural ally for their united Spanish realm. The two lands had much in common – above all, a deep suspicion of the country between them: rich, boastful France.

Henry's eldest son was only a year younger than Catherine, which made him the ideal match. And as luck would have it, he had been christened after the legendary king whose adventures had inspired minstrels in every corner of Europe.

His name was Arthur.

Catherine always knew her destiny lay in England. Her parents had signed the contract for her to marry young Arthur Tudor when she was just three.

Back then, you didn't get married just because you fell in love. For many people, marriage was a business deal, designed to make your family richer, more powerful and more respected.

For princes and princesses, contracts were often agreed when they were children. If, later on, the couple fell in love, that was a bonus. If not, they just had to get on with it.

Catherine had never been to England. But she knew it was cold and wet, a land of strange people, strange habits and even stranger food. She also knew the English spoke a weird language of their own invention, very unlike elegant European languages, such as Spanish.

When Catherine was twelve, Arthur's mother, Elizabeth of York, sent her some useful advice. Nobody in England spoke a word of Spanish, she said, so Catherine should learn some French, so that people would understand her. For some reason, it never occurred to anyone that she could just learn English.

Elizabeth's other tip was that Catherine should get used to drinking wine. 'The water of England,' she explained sadly, 'is not drinkable.'

By now, what had once seemed a very distant prospect was looming larger on the horizon. The future couple had even started sending each other love letters in Latin.

In October 1499, the thirteen-year-old Arthur told his fiancée that her letters made him so happy he imagined he was already kissing his 'dearest wife'. He could not wait to see her, and cherished the thought of her 'night and day'.

At this stage, Arthur had never even laid eyes on her. This was a kind of game, a ritual of courtly love, and they both knew it.

By now, King Henry was impatient to see his son's Spanish bride. But Ferdinand and Isabella dragged their feet, coming up with endless reasons why Catherine was not ready to travel.

Their other children had all left home, and they hated the thought of losing their youngest. 'Of all my daughters,' Ferdinand once told her, 'you are the one I love best.'

But by the spring of 1501 they had run out of excuses. Catherine was fifteen, and early one bright May morning, the day came.

The sun was high above the streets of Granada. The walls of the Alhambra glowed honey-pink. On the peaks of the Sierra Nevada, the snow glinted in the morning light.

Her travelling party was ready. An archbishop, a bishop, a nobleman and six young ladies were coming with her, all the way to England.

Now, as her companions waited on their horses, Catherine took one last look at the city she loved so much: the fountains and courtyards, the churches and mosques, the sweet-scented blossom, the softly murmuring fountains.

At last, she turned her horse's head and rode out of

the city, towards her new life. She would never see the Alhambra, Granada or her parents again.

Even for a princess, travelling abroad was an exhausting and dangerous business. And although Catherine had set out in the spring, to avoid the worst of the weather, her journey to England took her almost exactly half a year.

It took her three months to ride across the dusty plains to the port of La Coruña, in the far north-west of Spain. Wherever she passed, towns threw banquets and bullfights to honour their departing princess. And as Spain baked in the summer heat, her party slowed almost to a crawl.

Since Catherine had never travelled by sea before, she was understandably nervous. Before taking ship, she made a detour to the great church at Santiago de Compostela, supposedly the last resting place of Jesus's friend St James.

There, like so many Spanish knights before her, she knelt and prayed to the saint for a safe journey. Unfortunately, it turned out that St James was busy with other things.

The princess's ship left La Coruña on 25 August, packed with about sixty people. For the last time, Catherine waved farewell to her homeland – or so she thought.

But she had been at sea for barely a week when a ferocious storm blew up in the Bay of Biscay. Suddenly they found themselves driven off course, and in the end, the captain was forced to put in at Laredo, further along the Spanish coast.

Later, people said this had been an omen. Catherine, they claimed, had wondered aloud if the storm was a warning from God of 'some calamity' ahead.

But storms in the Bay of Biscay were hardly unusual, even in summer. Not even princesses were safe from the winds and waves that had swept so many sailors to their doom.

A month later, on the evening of 27 September, the gales died down and Catherine's captain was ready to try again. This time the voyage was much smoother – at least at first. But as they rounded the cape of Brittany into the English Channel, the weather turned against them.

What had started as a gentle breeze became a whipping wind, and then a howling gale. The ship pitched violently in the roiling waters. Hammer-blows of thunder shattered the heavens; towering waves hurled themselves onto the deck.

Huddled in her cabin, Catherine was racked with terrible seasickness. So were her terrified young companions, who sank to their knees in desperate prayer.

Fortunately, the captain knew his job. The plan had been for them to head for Southampton, supposedly the safest harbour in England, but he had a better idea.

So it was that at three o'clock on Saturday, 2 October

1501, Catherine's ship sailed into Plymouth, on the coast of Devon. She had landed more than a hundred miles west of where she was supposed to be. But the locals were delighted to see her, all the same.

Already a little crowd was waiting excitedly, eager for their first glimpse of the Spanish princess. And as Catherine stepped onto the quayside, cheers rang around the harbour.

'She could not have been received with greater rejoicing,' her doctor wrote to Isabella a few days later, 'had she been the Saviour of the world.'

So this was it: her new home, England. And right from the start, Catherine was determined to show all the dignity she had learned from her parents.

Exhausted after months of travelling, she was soaked and shivering, her clothes stained with seawater and sick. But before doing anything else, and without even bothering to change, she went straight to church.

And then, after she had offered prayers of thanks for her safe arrival, the girl from Castile began to explore her strange new country.

The Kingdom of Shadows

A week after she had landed, Catherine rode east, over the rolling hills and across a patchwork of cornfields and meadows.

In the autumn light the trees glowed russet-brown. Wood-smoke rose from the huddled villages. Over the fields drifted the sounds of hammer on anvil, scythe against whetstone.

To Catherine's eyes, England in 1501 was a strikingly damp, green country: a land of woods and hedgerows, oaks and beeches, manors and villages.

As she and her companions passed, the peasants stared at them with open curiosity. But when they called out to the travellers, Catherine could not understand a word they were saying.

She knew the English had a very high opinion of themselves. As one Italian traveller reported, they were 'a proud race without any respect, and claim they are superior to other nations'.

But to a girl used to the splendours of Granada, England was really not so impressive. With only two million people, this little kingdom was far smaller than superpowers such as France or Spain.

Its capital, London, had only 50,000 people.* And since nine out of ten people lived in the countryside, most of the places Catherine passed were tiny villages. Few of their wooden houses had more than two rooms.

As one visitor reported, English houses were disgustingly grubby, festering with 'spittle, vomit, dogs' urine and men's, too, dregs of beer and cast-off bits of fish, and other unspeakable kinds of filth'.

There was no running water, and the toilets were awful: a bucket, a hole in a plank or often just a hole in the ground, with a pile of leaves to clean yourself with afterwards.

As for the people, they were remarkably young. By and large, people lived only until their early forties, although a few lived much longer.

About a quarter were children under the age of ten – although with disease rampant, one in five children died before their first birthday.

For those who survived, life had its pleasures. Children played with dolls, footballs, hoops and marbles, and everybody loved music and dancing.

But from the time they could walk and talk, children lived in a world of strict rules. Beatings were common, and schools were fearsomely severe.

---

* In other words, Catherine of Aragon's London was no bigger than a medium-sized town today: say, Banbury, Yeovil, Durham or King's Lynn. The other Tudor cities were no bigger than very small towns.

The school day started at dawn and lasted until nightfall. There were lessons every day, except for Sundays.

Children sat on wooden benches, learning subjects such as Latin and Greek. If you stepped out of line, the teacher beat you with a stick – though if your parents were rich enough, they might pay for a 'whipping boy' to take the beatings for you.

Most children, however, did not go to school. From the age of seven, girls usually helped their mothers around the house, to build the fire and cook the dinner, while boys looked after the pigs, cows and sheep.

But as Catherine knew, the life of a princess was different. While the peasants struggled to make ends meet, princes and bishops wore splendid clothes with gold thread and glittering jewels.

They built enormous mansions, filled with tapestries, paintings and carpets. And while most people survived on coarse bread, cabbages and soup, they stuffed themselves with colossal quantities of meat and fish.

At banquets, rich people typically dined on beef and lamb, veal and venison, larks and storks, partridges and pheasants, followed by cod, herrings, salmon and eels. With no fridges to keep it cool, the meat often tasted pretty rotten, so their cooks covered it in spices to mask the taste.

Rich and poor had very different ideas of fun, too. As a princess, Catherine could look forward to falconry, hunting and tennis. But for most men and women, fun meant drinking, archery or cock fighting.

For everybody, though, this could be a cold, dark, dirty

world. Roads were muddy, villages were strewn with rubbish and people thought nothing of emptying their filthy chamber pots into the street.

Crime was common, and punishment brutal. Thieves were hanged, poisoners boiled alive and beggars branded with a red-hot iron.

And if you challenged King Henry, his vengeance was terrible.

Two years earlier, a young man called Edward, Earl of Warwick, had been led onto Tower Hill in London and forced to kneel before the executioner. A moment later, his severed head was raised before the crowd.

Edward's crime was to have been born a Plantagenet, a nephew of Richard III, giving him a claim to Henry's throne. As Catherine knew, the king had ordered his death to please her parents, showing them that his grip would never weaken.

It was a reminder that no matter how high you climbed, you could never be free from the shadow of the axe. And many years later, Catherine wondered if her own 'miseries and disasters' were God's punishment for the fate of this young man.

After three weeks on the road – and almost six months after she had left Granada – Catherine's little party clattered to a halt outside the manor house at Dogmersfield, Hampshire. Here she was due to rest for a couple of nights before the last push towards London.

But there was a surprise for the Spanish princess. Only a few hours later, a messenger arrived to say that King Henry was tired of waiting and was riding to meet her.

At first, Catherine was shocked. Meeting before the wedding broke all the rules of the Spanish court. But perhaps, deep down, she was also frightened to meet such a powerful figure alone, without her parents.

As she knew, old Henry Tudor was not a man to take lightly. After seizing the crown at Bosworth, he had ended decades of conflict and brought order to England. He had cracked down mercilessly on the powerful barons, hammering them with taxes that swelled his own coffers with gold.

To govern his kingdom, he relied on 'new men' – bishops, spymasters, lawyers and scholars – who owed him their unswerving loyalty. But he believed it was safer to be feared than loved.

Henry was a man of secrets and shadows. He knew that his enemies had their eyes on his crown and that they were waiting for a chance to strike.

So far, he had crushed three major rebellions and had been forced to execute some of his own relatives. He never dropped his guard, and never slept easily at night.

Above all, he was determined to secure the future of the Tudor dynasty. He knew that with one false step, England's stability would be undone, and his family name erased from history.

That was why Catherine was such a prize. She was not just his son's future bride, she was a future mother of Tudor kings.

No wonder, then, that Henry could not wait to see her. He was still in his riding gear when he arrived, his boots splattered with mud. But he came straight up to her chamber, waving aside her servants' protests.

For a split second they stared at each other, the English king and the Spanish princess. Some girls might have quailed before his searching gaze – but not Catherine of Aragon.

She saw a lean, weather-beaten man, with a watchful, fox-like face. He saw a short, fresh-faced girl of sixteen, with thick honey-coloured hair and solemn blue eyes.

Then Henry nodded and smiled. She was perfect, just as her parents had promised.

Late that afternoon, another visitor rode to Dogmersfield. For the first time, Catherine laid eyes on the young man to whom she had been promised for so long: the fifteen-year-old Arthur, Prince of Wales.

Arthur had the same lean frame, thin-lipped features and watchful eyes as his father. Serious and well read, he was a fine archer and an excellent dancer. All in all, Catherine could have done an awful lot worse.

There was only one drawback. When the shy young couple were left alone together, they tried to talk in Latin. But they had learned to pronounce the words differently, so Catherine struggled to understand what Arthur was saying.

But there was no reason to worry. They had years to get to know each other, after all.

When Catherine awoke on Thursday, 11 November, it was raining. It was always raining in this strange, cold island, she thought. How would she ever get used to it?

Today had been set aside for her grand entrance into King Henry's capital, London, but even the English could only put up with so much rain. She would have to wait until the next day, when the skies might be brighter.

So it was not until Friday morning that the Spanish party rode east through the orchards along the River Thames, glancing anxiously at the dark clouds overhead.

Catherine wore a neat hat, held on with gold lace, with her glossy hair cascading down her back. Instead of being carried by litter, as was the English custom, she rode into town on her richly decorated mule, like a true Castilian lady.

As she approached Southwark, she could see her mounted English escort waiting in the distance. One figure, straining eagerly to see the Spanish princess, stood out – if only because he was so much shorter than the others.

He was a boy, about ten years old, with fair, reddish hair and narrow blue eyes. He had a round, broad face, which lit up when he grinned. And even in the saddle he was bursting with energy, like a dog straining to be allowed off the leash.

This was the king's younger son, Henry, Duke of York. It was his job to bring his brother Arthur's wife into the capital, and he could hardly wait.

Now he and Catherine turned their horses north, towards the ancient bridge leading over the muddy Thames. The bridge was an extraordinary sight, creaking beneath the weight of its gatehouses and shops.

Beyond rose the steeples of London. The narrow lanes were packed with onlookers, the buildings decorated with silks and tapestries to welcome the Spanish princess.

Already, Catherine could see that it was nothing like Granada. The wooden houses were so tightly packed, their upper storeys jutting out over the pavements, that they blocked out the sunlight.

Instead of the sweet smell of orange blossom, the streets stank of drains and dung. She saw beggars calling for coins in the gutters, pigs roaming for scraps among the rubbish, men squatting to relieve themselves in the shadows.

Catherine's horse clattered over the bridge into the crowded maze. From Gracechurch Street she turned into Cornhill, riding past the jewellery shops of Cheapside towards St Paul's Cathedral. And there she said farewell to her young escort, slipped down from the saddle and retired to the Bishop's Palace, where her guest rooms had been prepared.

She had made a tremendous impression. 'Never, to my knowledge, has there been such a reception anywhere,' a law student called Thomas More wrote to his friend. 'But the Spanish escort – good heavens! What a sight! If you had seen it, I am afraid you would have burst with laughter; they were so ludicrous.'

To More, most of the Spaniards looked like 'hunchbacked, undersized, barefoot pygmies'. But the princess was different.

'Ah, but the lady!' he gushed. 'Take my word for it, she thrilled the hearts of everyone; she possesses all those qualities that make for beauty in a very charming young girl.'

Thomas More could hardly have known that one day, his devotion to Catherine of Aragon would cost him his life.

Two days later, in the cool air of an autumn morning, Catherine stepped out of the Bishop's Palace into the wide cathedral yard.

Already, the square was packed. There was nothing London loved more than a royal wedding, and the pavements were crammed with people, staring unashamedly at their new princess and jabbering away in their strange language.

There was one familiar face, though. Once again the boisterous little figure of Henry, Duke of York, had been chosen to escort Catherine into the cathedral. And slowly, solemnly, they began to walk.

Catherine's mind was a blur. All her life had led to this moment. This was the reason she had come to England. This was the day she had dreamed about for so long, her wedding day.

Knowing that thousands of eyes would be on her, she had dressed to make an impact. She wore a long satin gown in white and gold, ballooning out over a great hooped skirt, known as a farthingale. Over her face she wore a long silk veil, bordered with gold, pearls and jewels.

As she stepped through the great west door, St Paul's was heaving with spectators, squeezed into every corner. The Spanish trumpeters blared out a fanfare, and gasps of admiration rose from the congregation.

Catherine looked stunning, a vision of style and colour in cold, grey London. None of the spectators had ever seen anything like it. And on the wedding stage, Arthur's pride was plain for all to see.

Three hours later, the newly married Catherine, Princess of Wales, walked back down the raised walkway and through the cheering crowd. But her duties were not over yet. Now came the great wedding banquet, where she had been placed at the right hand of the King himself.

No expense had been spared. Everywhere you looked, reported one guest, you saw 'jewel-encrusted goblets' and 'dishes of purest gold', as well as the finest wine and food imaginable.

For Catherine, tired after her day in the spotlight, it was an overwhelming experience. But finally, long after darkness had fallen, it was time for bed.

Shyly, nervously, Catherine and Arthur made their way to their ceremonial bedchamber, accompanied by a procession of friends, relatives, bishops and noblemen. The bishops sprinkled the bed with holy water and murmured a prayer, asking God to give them healthy children and a long life.

And then, at last, the others withdrew. The door closed, and Arthur blew out the candle. Slowly, gently Catherine's thoughts faded into shadows. And with her English husband by her side, she fell asleep.

For two weeks the celebrations continued, a dizzying whirl of balls and banquets, jousts and pageants.

Although few people could take their eyes off the Spanish princess, one of the guests did his best to steal the show. Young Henry of York was clearly itching to have a turn in the limelight.

Late one night, the boy took to the dance floor with his twelve-year-old sister, Margaret. The musicians struck up a tune, which was much too slow for the excitable ten-year-old.

In open defiance of the court rules, young Henry ripped off his gown and started leaping madly about in his shirt.

Some of the guests were shocked, but the King and Queen were laughing too much to be angry with him.

The nights drew in. The air was colder now, and frost sparkled on the ground.

Slowly but surely, the party season was drawing to a close. On 29 November Catherine bade a sad farewell to the companions who had come with her from Spain. It was time for most of them to go home.

With them they carried a letter from Arthur to her parents. He promised to be a good husband, and assured them that he had 'never felt such joy in his life as when he beheld the sweet face of his bride'.

Catherine and Arthur stayed a little longer in London, but soon it was time for them to leave, too. A few days before Christmas they set off into the gathering gloom. And after days in the saddle, they reached the mist-wreathed hills of Shropshire.

Through the winter drizzle, Catherine caught her first glimpse of her new home, the great grey castle of Ludlow. Founded centuries earlier, it stood high on a rock above the river, its stern stone towers commanding the rolling borderlands between England and Wales.

Although this bleak fortress was very different from the garden paradise of the Alhambra, it was a magnificent building – a real-life Camelot, with thick walls, high battlements, a satisfyingly dark dungeon and a huge wood-floored Great Chamber.

Catherine's quarters were as richly decorated as any princess could want. And despite its forbidding appearance,

Ludlow could be a place of warmth and song, especially when the cups brimmed with wine, the minstrels played in the shadows and the flames danced in the great hearth.

For Arthur's young bride, the best days lay ahead. Although she and her husband did not yet speak the same language, they were only teenagers. And they were both sensible, dutiful people, determined always to do their best.

As winter gave way to spring, all the signs were good. One day Arthur would be a great king, with Catherine as his graceful queen. They would have children; they would be happy.

And then Easter came, and the wheel of fortune turned.

It had been a dark, miserable spring, the clouds glowering with the threat of thunder.

In the rain-soaked villages, men said the sweating sickness was abroad again. First came the chills, then the fever. Then, as your breath failed you, came the angel of death.

It all happened devastatingly quickly. As one writer put it, you could be 'merry at dinner and dead at supper'.

As Easter approached, Arthur fell ill. At first it seemed

nothing, but on Easter Sunday he retreated to his bedchamber, his body shivering uncontrollably, his eyes unnaturally bright, his brow slick with sweat.

For a week Arthur fought for life. But on Saturday, 2 April, he died. He was still only fifteen years old.

A few weeks later, as torches burned in the gloom, Arthur's men carried their young lord's coffin down from the castle. It was a grey, grim day: 'the foulest cold, windy and rainy day,' one reported, that he had ever known.

High above, as the wind howled at the castle towers, a tear-stained face stared bleakly down. At the age of sixteen, Catherine had become a widow.

Trapped in this cold, dark country, more than a thousand miles from home, she was on her own.

3

Catherine Alone

With the death of her teenage husband, Catherine collapsed. For days she lay on her bed, pale and sick, her body shivering with fever, her mind numb with grief.

For a while, her servants were seriously worried about her. But at last, when she was well enough to travel, she was helped into a litter, draped in black velvet, and carried slowly back south.

Only six months earlier she had ridden into London to the cheers of a welcoming crowd. Now she found the capital silent and closed, a city mourning its lost prince.

On King Henry, the news of Arthur's death had fallen like a hammer-blow. But he did not forget about the teenage princess, and Catherine was given rooms in Durham House, a grand palace overlooking the Thames.

There, cooped up with her Spanish servants, she spent the long days weeping, praying and reading her Bible. What, she asked, had she done to deserve this? What sins had she committed, to make God punish her so harshly?

But while Catherine struggled with her sorrow and misery, King Henry sat deep in thought.

He was in his mid-forties, and he was tired. The burdens of power, the secrets and suspicions, had taken their toll. He knew he might not have long left.

When he died, the crown would pass to young Henry, who was now just eleven. With so many rivals lurking, that could mean civil war and the end of the Tudor dynasty.

And what if something happened to young Henry before that? The old King would be left with no male heir, and all his efforts would have been for nothing.*

There was an obvious solution. Young Henry must have a wife from one of the most powerful families in Europe, who would in time bear him a son of his own. And there was an obvious candidate, right here in London – Catherine of Aragon.

The only problem was that Catherine had been married to Arthur. The Bible clearly stated that for a man to marry his 'brother's wife' was against God's law, which seemed to rule out the king's plan.

But there were ways around it. Slightly confusingly, another section of the Bible said that if a married man died without having children, his widow actually *ought* to marry his brother.

---

* He did have two daughters, but no woman had ever ruled England unchallenged. Henry I tried to leave the crown to his daughter, Matilda. But when he died in 1135, her cousin Stephen seized power instead, launching a long civil war.

That was the loophole the King needed. In the summer of 1503 he secured special permission from Pope Julius II, the head of the Roman Catholic Church. And on 25 June, Henry and Catherine were formally betrothed.

Since Henry was so young, the actual marriage would have to wait till he was fourteen. Technically, that meant he could still change his mind.

But as a woman, Catherine was just a pawn, at the mercy of her all-powerful father-in-law. Forbidden from returning to Spain, she had no option but to kick her heels in London until King Henry decided the time was right. And if he got a better offer, she would be thrown aside like a spare part.

In effect, Catherine was trapped, a prisoner in her London palace. And there was nothing at all she could do about it.

At the English court, life gradually returned to normal. Cautious, calculating King Henry went back to his account books, relentlessly heaping up gold in his treasure chests.

Meanwhile, his boisterous young successor was moved into an apartment next door to his father's chambers. There, young Henry was kept under constant guard, to make sure nothing untoward would befall him.

And all the time, in her townhouse by the river, a ghostly figure in black knelt alone, brooding in prayer.

Catherine was still a teenager, but her future had been torn away from her. Most days she saw nobody, apart from her Spanish servants. Even her parents seemed to have forgotten her. It was as if she had ceased to exist.

Although she was still a princess, she had little money. Writing home to Spain, she complained that she was so short of clothes she was 'all but naked', and had been forced to sell her bracelets to buy herself a black gown.

Above all, she was desperately lonely. Five years after she had come to this cold, grey country, she still could not understand a word of English. Trapped in her London house, the rain pouring endlessly down, she thought of the days when she had strolled with her parents in the Alhambra gardens, and cried herself to sleep.

Under the strain, her health was cracking. Her face was deathly pale, and she ate virtually nothing. Many people suspected that in her misery, she was deliberately starving herself, as if to punish herself for her sins. King Henry was so concerned that he arranged for the Pope to send her a stern letter, ordering her to eat and to stop tormenting herself.

And then fortune's wheel took another cruel turn. After months arguing with Catherine's father about her living expenses, King Henry ran out of patience. In June 1505, he ordered his son to break off the engagement and began scouring Europe's marriage market for a new bride.

Now Catherine's spirits sank to oblivion. All hope had vanished. Even her servants began to desert her, slinking, one by one, back to Spain.

The months passed, and things got worse. By late 1508 King Henry had opened talks for his son to marry the nine-year-old Eleanor of Austria – who, to add insult to injury, was Catherine's niece.

As Catherine marked her twenty-third birthday, she looked back on seven years of illness, grief, loneliness and depression. Everything had gone wrong. And what did she have to look forward to? Nothing.

In a last, tear-stained letter, written on 9 March 1509, she begged her father to bring her home, so she could end her 'few remaining days in serving God'.

'Do not let me perish,' she implored him. For if things went on as they were, she was 'afraid I might do something which neither the King of England nor Your Highness will be able to prevent'.

Perhaps not even Catherine herself knew what she meant by those words. But there was no mistaking the desperation behind them.

And then, a few weeks later, she heard stunning news. God had heard her prayers. King Henry was dead, and everything had changed.

Haggard and weary, Henry had been ill for years. At the beginning of 1509 he had shut himself away at Richmond Palace, his body wracked with coughing.

By early April it was obvious that the end was near. On the 20th the dying King summoned his personal confessor, and with tears in his eyes he confessed his sins.

The first Tudor monarch died late on the night of Saturday, 21 April. Yet even in death, he remained a man of secrets.

For two days, life at court went on as normal. The royal councillors came and went with fixed smiles, as if the old king was still alive, while his son Henry acted as if nothing had changed.

But behind closed doors, the seventeen-year-old heir was moving fast. To see off any prospect of revolt, he needed the support of his father's councillors, but that came at a price.

To do his dirty work, the old king had relied on two clever, ambitious lawyers, Richard Empson and Edmund Dudley. They had kept the grand families in check, but now the noblemen wanted their heads.

Young Henry did not hesitate. On 24 April, the day he was proclaimed king, Empson and Dudley were charged with treason and dragged to the Tower of London.

The two men protested that they had simply been following his father's orders, which was true. But young Henry wanted a fresh start, so they had to go.

Some people might have seen this as a sign of what was coming. The secrets and lies; the sudden, horrified realization; the grim-faced guards; the clang of the cell door; the interrogators, the torturers, the shadow of the scaffold – in the next thirty years, all these would become terrifyingly familiar.

But at the time, most people were too busy cheering their new teenage king to notice.

On paper, the young Henry VIII seemed the ideal modern monarch. Bright and curious, he was fluent in French and Latin, spoke a little Italian and Spanish, and was well versed in history, poetry and the classics. He knew the Bible closely and was fascinated by maps and scientific inventions.

He was an excellent musician, who could play the recorder, the lute and the harpsichord, and enjoyed writing his own songs. And he was a superb sportsman, who loved to spend hours hunting, jousting and playing tennis.

Above all, young Henry looked the part. 'The King is the handsomest prince I ever set eyes upon,' wrote one Italian ambassador, who thought his 'round face so very beautiful that it would become a pretty woman'.

That was an odd way of putting it, because Henry was the very picture of a great hero-king. He was more than six feet tall, broad-shouldered and strong, his red-gold hair shining in the spring sunlight.

At a time when people were smaller than they are today, this big, boisterous man towered over his subjects. It was no wonder, then, that so many saw him as a reborn King Arthur, who would lead England into a glittering new era.

As the Spanish ambassador reported, nobody wept for Henry's father. Instead, he remarked, 'they show so much pleasure that it is as if everyone had been let out of prison'.

Yet even now, at the dawn of Henry's reign, there was a hint of a darker side.

In moving so swiftly against Empson and Dudley, Henry had showed ruthless cunning. And even when his position was safe, there was no pity for his father's old servants.

For almost a year, Henry left the two men to rot in the Tower. Then, bored with listening to their appeals for mercy, he decided to get rid of them.

On 17 August 1510, the two men were taken out onto Tower Hill and publicly beheaded. The young king was not there to see it, though, because he was out hunting.

For Catherine, the new order brought a stunning transformation. At a stroke, her days of lonely waiting were over.

Like his father, young Henry was determined to secure the future of the Tudor dynasty. He needed a son as soon as possible; and for that, he needed a wife.

In another sign of things to come, Henry moved quickly. Once he had made up his mind, there was no shifting him.

On the morning of 11 June 1509, barely seven weeks into the new reign, Catherine rode to Greenwich Palace, on the south bank of the Thames. There, in front of a handful of guests, the Spanish princess and the English king were quietly married.

Twelve days later, Catherine returned to London in triumph, carried through the cheering throng on a litter drawn by two white horses. She was dressed in pure white satin, her rich honey-coloured hair long and loose, her head encircled by gleaming pearls.

On Midsummer Day she was crowned alongside her husband at Westminster Abbey. It seemed a magical day, a day of patriotic excitement and national rebirth. There were bonfires and banquets, parades and parties, tournaments and wine fountains.

For Catherine, it was like a dream: the crowds, the smiles, the golden crown, and perhaps above all, the sight of her new husband, tall and handsome in his robes of crimson velvet. It had all happened so suddenly – and yet it was all wonderfully real.

Once again, the young lawyer Thomas More was among the crowds, just as he had been when Catherine married Arthur. And once again, More was swept up in the emotion of the hour.

England, he wrote, stood on the brink of a new golden age. With the 'fiery power in his eyes' and the 'beauty in his cheeks', Henry VIII was a model of vigorous leadership. As for the queen, 'she will be the mother of kings as great as her ancestors'.

'This day,' wrote More, 'is the end of our slavery, the fount of our liberty, the end of sadness, the beginning of joy.'

For Catherine, these were indeed days of joy. After the long, empty years of depression, her prayers had been answered.

She was a queen, before whom men bowed with solemn respect. She had money, palaces, fine clothes and friends. And, above all, she had a handsome, dashing young husband – the kind of man she had dreamed about in the gardens of Granada.

No longer did she write to her father, Ferdinand, begging to come home. Instead, she wrote of her delight at her new life with a husband she adored.

Henry wrote to her father, too, assuring him that he was head over heels in love. He had 'rejected all other ladies in the world' to marry Catherine, and admired her more every day. Indeed, if asked to choose again, he would pick Catherine before any other woman on earth.

Henry meant every word. Deep down, beneath the boasting and showing-off, he had a starry-eyed, romantic streak.

Like Catherine, he had grown up reading about the Knights of the Round Table. Like her, he had always imagined himself as the hero of a glorious love story. And now, at last, his dream had come true.

Life seemed an endless whirl of fun and games. As Henry told Catherine's father, they spent their days enjoying 'continual feasts', as well as 'jousts, birding, hunting and other innocent and honest pastimes'.

Henry's greatest passion was for court masques, in which he and his friends would dress up in elaborate disguises. Catherine had to pretend that she did not recognize him. Then, when he whipped off his mask to reveal his true identity, her job was to gasp with amazement and admiration.

One Christmas, she was apparently so impressed that she invited the masked men to dance in her private chamber, and then covered her grinning husband with adoring kisses.

On another occasion, Henry and his rich friends dressed up as Robin Hood and his Merry Men before bursting into his wife's rooms. Pretending not to recognize them, Catherine and her ladies-in-waiting agreed to dance with the intruders, and once again the evening ended in giggles and kisses.

All the time, the couple waited for good news. And in the autumn of 1510 it came. Catherine was expecting a baby.

As Christmas approached, the royal court was a hive of activity. The King had ordered reams of purple velvet for his child's nursery. For the heir to the Tudor crown, everything must be perfect.

On New Year's Eve Catherine felt the baby stir, and knew the moment had come. A few hours later, just after the bells had rung in the New Year, her child was born. God had blessed her with a son.

It was one of the happiest moments of her life. All her waiting, all her misery had been worth it. She had given

Henry his heir; she had united England and Spain; she had fulfilled her destiny.

At the Tower of London, the cannons boomed out their salutes. In the streets of the capital, bonfires burned in the darkness.

The baby was named Henry, after his father and grand-father. One day, he would succeed them as king, ruling as Henry IX.

Henry was beside himself with joy. After making a thanksgiving pilgrimage to the shrine of the Virgin Mary at Walsingham, he organized a spectacular two-day tour-nament, with his wife in the place of honour.

The King was the star of the show, naturally. He called himself 'Sir Loyal Heart', and his horse was decorated with golden hearts to match the hearts adorning Catherine's gilded pavilion.

Again and again he charged down the jousting lists. Nobody could unseat him. And on the second day, when his adoring wife awarded him the trophy, they seemed the perfect couple, blessed and rewarded by God.

And then, just ten days later, the wheel turned again.

On 22 February, the baby died. Catherine was heart-broken. Her husband assured her that they had plenty of time for more sons. But even as they grieved for their little boy, the skies were darkening.

Hundreds of miles away, far across the sea, great armies were marching to fire and slaughter. The battle drums were beating, and England was going to war.

4

The Fields of Blood and Gold

The summer of 1513 was wet and gloomy. At Richmond Palace, Catherine sat quietly with her ladies, stitching her husband's shirts and listening to the rain pattering on the windowpanes.

Henry had been gone since the end of June, leading his troops across the Channel against the French. In the meantime, Catherine was in charge, with instructions to watch out for raiders from the neighbouring kingdom of Scotland, in the far north.

The Scots had been allied to the French for centuries: as Catherine knew, they could strike at any moment.

The weeks went by, and she waited for news. Every night she prayed for her husband's safe return. In the meantime, she had ordered the fleet to sail north, just in case.

And then, one day, news came. The Scottish king, James IV, was riding south from Edinburgh with the largest army people had ever seen. On 22 August, the Scots crossed the River Tweed, capturing castle after castle. The north of England seemed prostrate before them.

Catherine did not flinch. The daughter of a warrior queen, she relished the chance to show her fighting spirit. On her command, horsemen raced across the kingdom with a single message: 'England, awake!'

On 8 September she rode in splendour from Richmond Palace. On her head she wore a glittering golden helmet. Above her flew the banners of England and Spain.

Yet, even as Catherine began the journey north, the moment of decision was at hand. The very next day, her chief commander, the Earl of Surrey, caught up with the Scots on the marshy fields of Flodden, not far f   Tweed.

The Scots had the higher ground, greater nur the latest weapons: long, merciless pikes, as well twenty heavy guns. Their victory seemed a conclusion.

But as the Scottish cannons thundered in the afternoon gloom, Surrey's men held firm. And as the Scottish king gazed grimly across the Flodden fields, he realized he would have to win this the old-fashioned way, hand-to-hand in the pouring rain.

At about four o'clock, James ordered his pikemen into battle. Stumbling down the slope, they smashed like a wrecking-ball into the English lines. The air echoed with the clash of metal on bone, the howls of the wounded and the shrieks of the dying.

Yet still the English refused to break. And it was now, with the outcome hanging in the balance, that James charged, leading his knights into the thick of the fighting.

As his horse crashed into the English line, James could see the Earl of Surrey, just yards away, but still out of reach. Everywhere men were screaming with rage, their swords rising and falling, bodies slipping and sliding in the mud.

But as the shock of their assault faded, James's men began to tire. The English archers were raining arrows into the Scottish rear. The Scots were no longer making ground; if anything, they were going backwards.

And suddenly, with savage fervour, the English surged. The Scottish line wavered – and broke. Against all the odds, they were beaten.

Darkness came, and the battlefield fell silent. On the sodden earth lay the mud-splattered, blood-soaked body of James, King of Scotland. Beside him lay the twisted corpses of almost every major Scottish lord, as well as ten thousand ordinary soldiers.

When the news reached Catherine, she could not contain her joy. She had promised her husband that she would keep his kingdom safe; and she had done it.

In a single afternoon, the Scottish threat had been destroyed for a generation. It was one of the sweetest moments of her life.

Flodden was just one bloody battle in a wider war, stretching from the moors of Northumberland to the mountains of Italy.

Europe was a continent in turmoil, scarred with battle-lines and siege-trenches. By the mid-1510s, the key players were two countries that Henry and Catherine knew very well.

One was England's age-old enemy, France, with its huge population and mighty army under the crafty Francis I. The other was the sprawling, gold-rich Holy Roman Empire of Catherine's nephew, Charles V, who had inherited the throne of Spain to add to his family's vast territories in Austria, Hungary, Italy, the Low Countries and central Europe.

England was not remotely rich enough to compete with these two great rivals, and Henry's father had always tried to stay out of European wars. But Henry was desperate to prove himself the equal of Francis and Charles. As his old tutor remarked: 'Our King is not after gold, or gems, or precious metals, but virtue, glory, immortality.'

Henry's romantic enthusiasm for knights and heroes had never faded. He loved competing in tournaments, knew all the details of England's great battles and adored the legends of the Knights of the Round Table. When the Emperor Charles visited England, Henry even paid for the repainting of a huge Round Table, which is still on show at Winchester Castle today.

Unfortunately for Henry, reality never quite matched his dreams. Despite England's victory at Flodden, the war in France ended in stalemate. And when it was all over, Henry was left with just two French towns as a reward for his efforts.

But the war had one important legacy. During his French campaign, Henry had come to rely on one particular councillor, who was remarkably good at managing the army, organizing supplies and dealing with England's allies.

Unlike most of the King's companions, Thomas Wolsey did not come from a noble family. He was a butcher's son from Ipswich, who had trained as a priest before becoming a royal official.

Wolsey was clever, ambitious and hard-working, a witty speaker and a brilliant organizer. Above all, he realized that the way to win Henry's favour was to do all the boring jobs for him. As he confided to his servant, his only goal was to 'advance the King's own will and pleasure', whatever that might be.

Wolsey's rise was dazzlingly swift. He only joined Henry's council in 1510, but by 1514 he had become Archbishop of York, the second most powerful man in the English Church.

A year later, the butcher's son became Lord Chancellor: in effect, the head of Henry's government. And in that same year, 1515, the Pope made him a cardinal, a prince of the worldwide Catholic Church.

Wolsey was now very grand indeed. When his red cardinal's hat arrived from Rome, he had it paraded through the streets of London, as if he were a monarch about to be crowned.

To the noble families, he was a jumped-up nobody. But Henry treated him as a friend, walking arm-in-arm with him in the royal garden, eagerly discussing his plans for the future.

As the years went by, Wolsey amassed ever more titles and honours. He collected paintings and sculptures, founded schools and colleges, and owned several country houses.

His most spectacular creation was Hampton Court, near Henry's palace at Richmond. Here he built a magnificent Italian-style mansion, with exquisite gardens and towering brick chimneys, which still draws thousands of visitors today.

Nothing like it had ever been seen in England before. It was no wonder people called him an *alter rex* – a second king.

While Cardinal Wolsey took care of the business of government, Henry took care of the business of pleasure. As Wolsey's servant recalled, the King much preferred to 'follow his desire and appetite', rather than focus on 'the busy affairs of this realm'.

That suited Wolsey perfectly. He could get on with

running the country, and Henry could get on with having fun.

Even the King's loud, swaggering friends found Henry exhausting company. He liked to rise early and spend his mornings jousting, shooting or hunting in the royal forests.

He loved music and tennis, riding and wrestling. He was always devising some elaborate new prank, dressing up for a masque or writing jokey love letters to some pretty girl.

Evenings meant feasting and dancing, cards and gambling . . . and so to bed, before leaping up to start all over again the next day.

Needless to say, this cost a lot of money. But as Henry saw it, life should be a glamorous spectacle, a glittering show.

When he wore jewels, they had to be the most dazzling money could buy. When he wore robes, they must be 'the richest and most superb that can be imagined'.

His wardrobe was a temple to extravagance. He owned 79 fur-trimmed gowns, 86 coats and 134 doublets, many of them made from velvet, silk or satin.

In a single year, he got through 200 shirts, 37 hats, 60 pairs of hose – like long socks – and 175 pairs of leather boots, satin shoes and velvet slippers. In today's money, his total clothes budget was about £80 million – *every single year*.

Then there were the rubies and diamonds, the perfumes and spice-boxes, the paintings and tapestries, the clocks and watches, the glass goblets and gold plates . . .

In the summer of 1520, Henry's love of luxury reached an awe-inspiring climax. With England and France finally at peace, Cardinal Wolsey had arranged a meeting with King Francis. Both men were determined to make it the event of the century.

As usual, Wolsey planned every detail. The meeting place – a meadow on the edge of the English-held territory in northern France – was chosen to make the greatest possible impact.

When the two kings arrived on 7 June, accompanied by crowds of courtiers, knights and servants, they found the countryside covered with spectacular tents, the gold-leaf decorations gleaming in the sun. There was a long tiltyard for tournaments, as well as enclosures for musicians, entertainers and wrestlers.

There was a gigantic timber-framed palace, its tented sides painted to look like stone and brick, with glass windows and a fully equipped kitchen. There were stunning fireworks, so loud they frightened some of the guests. There were two fountains, bubbling over with torrents of wine. There was even a chapel, with dozens of priests and two choirs.

Everywhere you looked, gold shimmered in the summer heat. People called it the Field of the Cloth of Gold, and never had a nickname seemed more fitting.

Once again, Catherine played her part to the full. She had brought so many servants that it took six wagons and forty carriages to move them around the site. Her attendants wore bright yellow doublets, orange boots and black velvet cloaks, and her horses' saddles were decorated with cloth of gold.

She had her own quarters, complete with gold candlesticks and silk tapestries. Here she entertained King Francis, who proved to be a model of flirtatious French charm.

There was feasting and jousting, falconry and archery, and Henry loved every minute of it. At one point he even challenged Francis to a wrestling match – which, with a characteristically sly manoeuvre, the Frenchman won.

On the final day, Henry and Francis swore undying friendship and vowed to build a chapel to Our Lady of Peace on that very spot. With that, the kings went home, the candlesticks were packed away and the tents were taken down.

And just two years later, as surely as autumn follows summer, England and France were at war again.

As Catherine sailed back across the Channel, the memory of her first landing at Plymouth could hardly have seemed more distant.

Nineteen years ago she had been cold and frightened, a teenage girl in a strange new land. But now, as queen, she had never been more popular. In every village in England, people talked of her kindness and charity.

No queen had ever taken her duties more seriously.

Whenever Henry pulled on his armour for another tourna-ment, she was always there, smiling with encouragement.

No household in the world, wrote the Dutch scholar Erasmus, offered 'so clear an example' of a happy marriage. And nowhere, he added, could you find 'a wife keener to match her admirable husband'.

Yet amid all this splendour, there was a shadow. For all Catherine's prayers, God had not given them the son they craved.

Year after year, she took to her bedchamber, convinced that this time would be different. But this was an age when many children died very young, and fate never seemed to be on her side.

At long last, in February 1516, she gave birth to a healthy little girl, whom she christened Mary. In public, Henry claimed to be delighted. But since no woman had ever ruled England unchallenged, few people seriously expected pale, solemn little Mary to become queen.

For Catherine, the lack of a son was a lasting sadness. But she told herself that it must be God's will; and in any case, after the trials of her teenage years, she was grateful to have her husband and daughter.

For Henry, though, it was different. To men with power and money, the survival of their family line mat-tered enormously. They saw themselves as links in a long chain, uniting those who were living, those who were dead, and those who were yet to be born.

If Henry died without a son, leaving the crown to the infant Mary, the Tudor dynasty would probably be over.

All his father's hard work, all his jewels and finery, would have been for nothing.

Deep down, Henry knew he would not live for ever. In 1514 he had suffered a nasty shock after coming down with measles. And when the sweating sickness swept through London a few years later, he fled into self-isolation in the countryside, changing houses every few days.

He also had an intense fear of plots and conspiracies. Even now, decades after the Battle of Bosworth, there were plenty of powerful lords with Plantagenet blood in their veins, who might easily be tempted to strike for the crown.

Like his father, he was always looking over his shoulder, always dreading the knife in the dark. And always, always, there was that missing son . . .

So the years went by, feasts and festivals, dances and tournaments.

Physically, Henry was in his prime. As the Venetian ambassador reported, he was 'much handsomer than any sovereign in Christendom'. It was the 'prettiest thing in the world' to watch him playing tennis, 'his fair skin glowing through a shirt of the finest texture'.

But what of Catherine? She was five years older than her husband, and in December 1525 she turned forty.

The years of teenage innocence were far behind her; the rigours of childbirth had taken their toll. To put it bluntly, she had got very fat.

Always quiet and serious, she was now more intense than ever. While her husband went off hunting and dancing, she retreated to her room, devoting herself to prayer and pilgrimage.

When the Spanish writer Juan Luis Vives arrived in England, she took him to pray at a riverside convent near Richmond Palace. As the royal barge carried them home, they discussed the turns of fortune's wheel.

If she had to choose between happiness and sadness, Catherine said thoughtfully, she would choose sadness. If you were too happy, it was easy to lose sight of what mattered. But even in the depths of sadness, you could always find consolation.

It was exactly what Vives expected to hear from such a serious-minded woman. But when he remembered her words years later, they had a darkly ironic ring.

For even as Catherine's barge glided through the water, her husband was deep in thought. Unlike his wife, Henry had never accepted that he would have no son.

Again and again it nagged at him. Who would wear the crown when he was gone? What would happen to the Tudor bloodline? And above all, why had God punished him so cruelly?

Slowly but surely, as he watched Catherine grow older,

an idea was taking root in Henry's mind. Perhaps God *was* punishing him. Perhaps he *had* done something wrong.

Perhaps it had been a sin to marry his brother's widow, all those years ago. Perhaps, in the eyes of God, she was not really his wife after all.

At first he said nothing. Catherine never suspected a thing. But as the weeks turned into months, the cloud in his mind became steadily darker.

And then, out of nowhere, something momentous happened. Henry fell in love.

5

The Fires of Faith

One day, when her daughter, Mary, was barely a year old, Catherine rode out of London, heading for the far eastern edge of England.

Her destination was the river port of Ipswich, which had grown rich from the cloth trade with the Continent. What had caught Catherine's interest, though, was the miraculous wooden statue of Our Lady of Grace.

Housed in a chapel just outside the town's western gate, this image of Jesus's mother, Mary, was one of the most popular tourist attractions in the country. Many people believed it had supernatural powers.

Only two years earlier, the statue had apparently cured a teenage girl, who had been suffering from terrible fits. The girl claimed that inside the chapel, she had seen a magical vision of Mary herself, who had cast out the demon possessing her.

In the wake of the story, thousands of visitors poured into Ipswich to see the shrine for themselves. Some wondered if the girl really had seen a vision; but as the local innkeepers counted their takings, they were in no mood to argue with her.

For Catherine, who took her faith so seriously, the trip to the shrine was an unforgettable experience. But the Ipswich statue was not unique.

Other towns across England had precious statues of the Virgin Mary, too. The most famous, the shrine of Our Lady of Walsingham, was one of the most visited tourist destinations in Europe, and Catherine went more than once.

To people in the sixteenth century, there was nothing strange about such trips. From the glimmers of dawn to the embers of dusk, faith and mystery were woven into their everyday lives.

From the moment they could talk, children knew about God's presence in the world. For help they prayed to Jesus, who had died on the cross but risen unconquered from the tomb.

In church they knelt before the saints of the Catholic Church, courtiers in the kingdom of heaven. But they lived in dread of the Devil, who was forever trying to tempt them into the fires of hell.

As Catherine knew, some people abroad prayed to a different god, like the Muslim Moors in her native Spain. For the English, though, there was only one true faith, set out in the Bible and embodied in the local church.

Richly decorated and brightly painted, the church was the heart of every village, the pride of the community. People gladly donated large sums of money towards a new spire or a stained-glass window. They were proud of their chalices and candlesticks, their gilded images of the saints and wooden carvings of Christ on the cross.

The Catholic Church was immensely powerful, with riches and authority far beyond the greatest nobleman. It employed tens of thousands of priests and bishops, serving parishes across the country.

The head of the English Church was the Archbishop of Canterbury. But he answered to the Pope in Rome, who had all the grandeur and authority of a king.

In theory, the Pope's dominion encompassed the earth. He was God's guardian of truth, ruthlessly punishing any criticism of the Church's ancient traditions.

For example, it was forbidden to question the Mass, the most important Catholic ritual of all. At every service the priest re-enacted the Last Supper, when Jesus had offered bread and wine to his disciples, explaining that they were his body and blood.

This re-enactment, the Mass, was so mysterious that the priest celebrated it alone at the altar, behind a carved wooden screen. Catholics believed that at the crucial moment, the bread and wine *literally* turned into the body and blood of Christ. This was the miracle of miracles, a daily reminder of the sacrifice God's Son had made to save mankind from evil.

To Henry's subjects, being saved from evil could hardly have been more urgent. Their priests told them that when they died, they would spend centuries in a place called

Purgatory, where they would pay for their misdeeds on earth.*

To most people, Purgatory sounded genuinely terrifying. Quite apart from the blazing fires, there would be all sorts of agonizing torture machines, as well as armies of demons with sharp skewers and red-hot pokers.

What was more, you might be trapped there for hundreds, even thousands of years. Only after you had paid the price for your sins would you be allowed into heaven.

But the picture was not entirely gloomy. For instance, you could turn for help to the saints: holy men and women whose lives had been models of Christian service.

According to the Church, the saints had miraculous powers. Even their images and relics – a bit of bone, a severed finger, a few drops of blood – were charged with magic and mystery. So every year, thousands of pilgrims descended on the most popular saints' shrines, hoping for supernatural help.

The other good news was that the Pope had the power to wash away your sins. If you carried out some good work for the Church – for example, by making a donation for a new spire, or giving money towards some golden candlesticks – then you would be rewarded with an 'indulgence'.

---

* Purgatory was similar to hell, but not the same. If you went to hell, you were stuck there for ever. Purgatory was a very miserable waiting room, before the delights of heaven.

Each indulgence wiped out some of your time in Purgatory. In return for your money, you got a certificate entitling you to skip a few thousand years of torment.

Even at the time, there were some people who thought this a blatant con. Could a piece of paper seriously get you out of Purgatory? How could it be right for the Pope to make money out of people's gullibility?

Sometimes, in darkened corners, you might hear people whispering that indulgences were a fraud, relics were a trick and the Pope was a liar.

You had to be careful, though. The Church had informers everywhere, searching for 'heretics' with dangerous views. The wrong word in the wrong ear, and you could find yourself being dragged off to prison, or even burned alive at the stake.

Of course, Catherine never dreamed of questioning the Pope. She had been raised as a strict Catholic, and any criticism of the Church filled her with horror.

To Catherine, indulgences were an essential part of God's universe, just like the power of the saints, the magic of relics and the miracle of the Mass. The Church was the only true faith, and the Pope's word was law.

So it had been in the past, and so it would be in the future. That would never change – would it?

A few months after Catherine had returned from Ipswich, the first rumours of rebellion arrived in England.

As snow flurried through the streets of London, visiting merchants reported strange goings-on in a small town in Germany. It had all started on the last day of October 1517, when the people of Wittenberg awoke to find that somebody had nailed a list of ninety-five 'theses', or opinions, to the great doors of the Castle Church.

When they crowded round to read the list, many people were shocked. Relentlessly, unsparingly, the theses attacked the idea that you could buy your way into heaven. The only way to win God's forgiveness, the paper said, was by being truly sorry, not by buying an indulgence from some fat priest.

The list's author was a little-known monk called Martin Luther, who had lost patience with what he saw as the greed and lies of the Catholic Church. It was nonsense, he said, that you could get into heaven by doing 'good works'. In reality, all that mattered was faith in God's holy word.

The Pope and his bishops were furious, because Luther was challenging the basis of their wealth and power. Soon, the Holy Roman Emperor, Charles V, declared him an outlaw and demanded his arrest.

But Luther could not care less. The Pope was a 'shameless, barefaced liar', who spent his time licking the Devil's bottom. In fact, according to Luther, all popes in history had been 'desperate, thorough arch-rascals, murderers, traitors, liars, the very scum of all the most evil people on earth'.

Talking like this could get you killed. But even as the

Emperor's agents launched a huge manhunt, Luther's ideas were spreading across Europe.

One of his first English readers was the lawyer Thomas More, a strict Catholic who had just joined King Henry's council. Although More was appalled by Luther's arguments, he was not especially worried. Surely, he thought, the English people would never listen to this rubbish!

But he was wrong. For in villages across southern England, hundreds of people were waiting for somebody like Luther to set off an explosion.

More than a century earlier, a scholar called John Wycliffe had claimed that the Catholic Church was misleading the English people, feeding them lies to keep them in their place.

Wycliffe and his followers, known as the Lollards, rejected popes and priests, relics and rituals, shrines and saints. They thought statues of the Virgin Mary should be used for firewood, and said the miracle of the Mass was nonsense.

Above all, they thought it was a disgrace that only priests who understood Latin could read the Bible. They wanted ordinary people to read it for themselves, in their own language.

The Church's agents had done their best to crush the Lollards. They arrested them, bullied them and burned them alive. Meanwhile, translating and reading the Bible in English were punishable by death.

But the Lollards survived. They went underground, meeting in secret to share their ideas.

They dreamed of an England free from priestly control,

where ordinary people could come together to read God's word. They saw themselves as a resistance movement, and waited patiently for the spark that would light the fire and burn the Catholic Church to the ground.

Now, with the arrival of Luther's ideas, they became bolder than ever. A Berkshire widow claimed that wooden images of saints were just 'carpenters' chips'. A man in London said the Mass was all rubbish. And a man in Buckinghamshire told pilgrims they were 'fools', and loudly urinated on the floor of the shrine while they were celebrating Mass.

Of course, these were only isolated, individual acts of rebellion. But when you put them together, they began to add up.

Eventually, the Pope's agents in England decided to send a message. One Sunday in May 1521, bishops gathered outside St Paul's Cathedral. After issuing a bloodcurdling warning against the 'thick black cloud' of Luther's ideas, they hurled copies of his books onto a bonfire.

But even King Henry knew that burning books is no way to win an argument. Henry had read Luther's works and violently disagreed with them. Now he decided to take on the German monk in a battle of ideas.

That summer, readers got their hands on *The Defence of the Seven Sacraments*, the first printed book ever written by an English monarch. Henry wrote much of it himself, although his friend Thomas More lent a hand, too.

It was a huge international hit, and a delighted Pope Leo

X awarded Henry the title of *Fidei Defensor* – 'Defender of the Faith'.*

But Luther scoffed at Henry's efforts. The English king, he declared, was 'a pig, an ass, a dunghill, the spawn of an adder, a basilisk, a lying buffoon and a mad fool with a frothy mouth'.

Since it was beneath Henry's dignity to bandy words with a German monk, he got More to do it for him. More duly called Luther an 'ape', a 'drunkard' and a 'scoundrel', and attacked his ideas as the 'muck which your damnable rottenness has vomited up'.

But Luther, who had such a talent for abuse himself, could easily cope with a few rude words. And far from being settled, the argument was only just beginning.

For as Henry returned to the pleasures of the hunt, a young English priest called William Tyndale was taking a last look at his native land from the deck of a ship, bound for Germany. And what Tyndale was planning was nothing short of revolutionary – a book that would change his country for ever.

---

* Ever since, every English and British monarch has used this title, and the initials FD still appear on pound coins today.

William Tyndale was not a powerful man. He was a tutor and preacher from a Gloucestershire village, who loved the word of God and thought people ought to be able to read it for themselves.

Tyndale knew he was flirting with danger, but he could not help himself. When an old priest told him that an English Bible would break the Pope's laws, he exploded: 'I defy the Pope and all his laws! . . . If God spares me, I will cause the boy who drives the plough to know more of the Bible than you do!'

Outbursts like this were terribly dangerous, and in the spring of 1524 Tyndale fled to Luther's homeland. In the city of Cologne, he found a printer who agreed to produce his English version of the New Testament, the section of the Bible telling the stories of Jesus and his disciples.

But even in Germany, Tyndale had to be careful. The Pope's spies and the Emperor's agents were everywhere, skulking in alleys, lurking in the shadows, always listening for whispers of rebellion.

Unfortunately for Tyndale, the printer liked to talk. One day he had a visitor, a polite, well-spoken man who said he wanted some work done. The stranger offered the printer a glass of wine, and as they chatted, the printer's tongue began to wag.

He knew a great secret, he said, 'by which all England was to be brought to the side of Luther'. Right now he was printing 3,000 copies of Tyndale's New Testament, which would soon be smuggled into the heart of Henry's kingdom.

The stranger smiled thinly, drained his glass and disappeared into the twilight. He had got the information he wanted.

A few days later, Imperial soldiers burst into the print shop. Racing to escape his pursuers, Tyndale had to make a desperate getaway. Clutching a half-finished text of his precious book, he leapt aboard a boat heading up the River Rhine.

Disembarking at the city of Worms, constantly looking out for imperial agents, the young priest eventually found another printer. And by the spring of 1526, Tyndale's New Testament was finally ready.

Slim enough to fit in your pocket, this was one of the most sensational books in English history. For the first time, ordinary people could read the story of Jesus in their own language, making sense of his message for themselves.

And Tyndale's book left a lasting mark on English itself. He wrote simply and clearly, using short, sharp words ordinary people would immediately understand.

It was this courageous man who invented many of the expressions we take for granted, from *signs of the times*, *let there be light* and *fall flat on his face* to *the land of the living*, *the parting of the ways* and *the twinkling of an eye*. Only one other man in history, the playwright William Shakespeare, has had such an impact on the language we speak today.

The first copies of Tyndale's book arrived in England in the autumn of 1526, hidden in wine barrels and bundles of cloth. Spluttering with rage, the Bishop of London condemned it as a 'pestiferous and most pernicious poison', and organized a massive book-burning on the steps of St Paul's.

But the slim, leather-bound volumes kept on coming. With new print shops opening across Europe, Tyndale and his supporters could make thousands of copies in cities like Worms and Antwerp before smuggling them across the sea into England.

By the following spring, the Archbishop of Canterbury was desperately asking his fellow bishops for money, so that his agents could buy up all the copies and destroy them. The Bishop of London even travelled to Antwerp and bought 6,000 copies from the printer, just so he could burn them.

But Tyndale's message was making converts all over England. For the first time, his Bible gave people a private, personal relationship with God. They no longer needed priests and rituals, shrines and relics. As Tyndale explained, you just had to read with an open mind, and you would be 'born anew' in the love of God. For many people, this was an extraordinarily exciting feeling.

And among the underground resistance, nicknamed 'Protestants', there was a real sense of enthusiasm now. Some no longer bothered to hide, as they once had. They handed out papers and pamphlets, shared illegal books and Bibles, and even smashed and defaced shrines and images.

By now, the leaders of the Church were becoming seriously worried. They had already seen Luther's ideas sweep through Germany. They could not let the same thing happen in England, too.

Desperate to fight back, the Bishop of London asked Thomas More to produce a counterblast. Once again, More took up his pen with gusto.

Smouldering with passion, More believed these new Protestants were no better than traitors. Tyndale, he wrote, was 'a hell-hound in the kennel of the Devil . . . discharging a filthy foam of blasphemies* out of his brutish beastly mouth'.

More prided himself on being a civilized man, but now he thirsted for fire and bloodshed. It was time, he wrote, to take off the gloves, and treat these heretics with the ruthlessness they deserved. Burning them in public was 'lawful, necessary and well done'.

When More thought of their death agonies, his heart surged with cruel delight. Their bodies would burn for only a few moments. But their souls, he wrote gleefully, were destined for hell, 'where the wretches burn for ever'.

But as More looked forward to the final victory over the Protestant heretics, a clever, spiky young woman was leafing eagerly through Tyndale's latest book.

Her name was Anne Boleyn. And within just a few years, she would bring Thomas More's world crashing down.

---

* Blasphemy is any kind of speaking or swearing that mocks religion or God.

6

The Lady of the Green Castle

It was the spring of 1522, and on the field of war England's king faced his destiny.

Tall and broad-shouldered, clad in blue and gold, Henry cut a magnificently imposing figure. By his side strode his finest knights and closest companions, a band of brothers worthy of the old Arthurian tales.

Ahead lay his target, the fabled Green Castle. In the distance Henry could see its soaring towers and fluttering banners.

As he came closer, the castle's guns opened fire. Missiles roared through the air, and the defenders howled their defiance.

It was a terrifying scene. Or it would have been, if the Green Castle's battlements had not been made from tin foil, and if the defenders had not been some of the court's prettiest young ladies.

The whole thing was a masque, a revel, organized by Cardinal Wolsey at his grand London house, York Place. It was the kind of entertainment Henry adored, and as the girls bombarded him with sweets and cakes, he hurled back a hail of oranges.

At last, after the 'fighting' had ended in stalemate, the ladies allowed themselves to be captured. Down they came, grinning and giggling. The court musicians struck up a tune, and the dancing began.

Eight ladies defended the Green Castle that day. Seven of them were well known at court. The eighth was a thin-faced, dark-eyed young woman, who had just come home after years in the French court.

Her friends called her Nan. But we remember her as Anne Boleyn – the woman who stole the heart of a king, and changed the course of England's history.

At the time of the Green Castle siege, Anne Boleyn was twenty-one. Born in Norfolk, she was the daughter of one of Henry's most accomplished diplomats, Sir Thomas Boleyn.

A careful, business-like man, Sir Thomas had a fine ear for languages. That made him useful to the King, who used him as a go-between with foreign princes.

As a result, Anne had spent much of her life abroad. When she was twelve she accompanied her father to

Brussels. A few months later he sent her to Paris, where she became a maid to the French queen.

For the rest of her teenage years, Anne remained in Paris. She spoke fluent French, learned French music and dressed in the latest French style. She read French translations of the Bible and absorbed the new ideas about God and the Church.

At the end of 1521 she was recalled to England, where she landed a new post as one of Catherine's ladies-in-waiting. With her Continental poise she made an instant impression, although many people regarded her as a Frenchwoman in all but name.

Nobody ever described Anne Boleyn, with her thick black hair, sallow skin, long neck and lean face, as a great beauty. But they were impressed by her deep, dark eyes: 'black and beautiful', wrote the Venetian ambassador. With one flutter, agreed another observer, Anne could convey the entire 'secret testimony of the heart'.

Above all, Anne had personality. She was a well-read woman who was never afraid of an argument. She danced, sang and played the lute beautifully. She was quick and sharp, with a flashing wit and a waspish tongue.

True, she had a fiery temper, and could be mocking and vindictive. But to her admirers, she seemed a woman of spirit.

Among them was the poet Thomas Wyatt, who fell for her at court. In one poem, Wyatt imagined himself as a huntsman and Anne as a deer: wild, beautiful and always just out of reach.

The poem ends with an image of the deer's collar.

There, engraved 'with diamonds in letters plain', are the mysterious words: '*Noli me tangere*, for Caesar's I am.'

Noli me tangere is Latin for 'Do not touch'. And it's not hard to work out whom Wyatt meant by Caesar. He meant King Henry.

Perhaps not even Henry himself was quite sure when he fell in love with Anne Boleyn. But by the spring of 1526, just over four years after she had returned from France, he was smitten.

He had had sweethearts before, including Anne's older sister, Mary. Catherine was not exactly overjoyed about it, but she knew this was how kings behaved.

But Henry's obsession with Anne was different. Part of it was that she was so different from Catherine: younger, sharper, wittier, spikier.

He could not get her out of his head. And all the time she drew him on, knowing exactly when to tease and toy with him, and when to push him away.

Soon he was scribbling love notes, a very unusual thing for a king to do. He often left them in books, like a teenager writing messages in his school textbook.

'I am yours. Henry R* forever,' he wrote in one prayer book, below a picture of Jesus. And Anne replied with a little poem, perfectly chosen to appeal to his romantic side:

By daily proof you shall me find
To be to you both loving and kind.

---

* R stands for *Rex*, which is Latin for 'King'.

By early 1527 Henry was bombarding her with letters. He claimed he had been 'struck with the dart of love', and was in a 'great agony' to know if she felt the same.

He wrote in riddles and codes, which only the two of them understood, and which nobody else has ever been able to crack:

B.N.R.I. de R.O.M.V.E.Z.
V. N. A. 1. de A. o. na. v. e. r.

And like a lovestruck schoolboy, he signed off with a heart enclosing the initials AB and HR, and a motto in French: 'I seek no other.'

Calling himself Anne's 'loyal servant', he begged her to surrender to him, 'body and soul'. If she agreed, she would be his only love. He would 'cast off all others', and 'serve you and you alone'.

Almost anybody else would have accepted. And if she had, the course of English history might have been completely different.

But Anne did not want to be the king's mistress. She had much loftier ambitions. She wanted to be his queen.

The spring of 1527 was wet and cold. Food was scarce, and farmers feared a dreadful harvest.

In the countryside, children were starving. In London, so many people queued for bread that some were crushed to death. And now there were reports that the sweating sickness had returned, carrying off young and old alike.

As rain poured down from a dull slate sky, Henry sat alone, lost in contemplation.

He desperately wanted a son, but fortune had not granted him one. Why not? God must be punishing him for marrying his brother's widow.

And then there was Anne. He loved her; he was sure of it. What agony it would be to let her go! But he could not marry her. Unless . . . unless . . .

In the sixteenth century, divorce was almost unheard of – but only *almost*. A king could get an annulment, if the Pope agreed that he had not been properly married in the first place.

Again and again Henry looked at the crucial passage in his Bible, which said it was 'unclean' for a man to marry his brother's wife. Back when he was a boy, the old Pope, Julius II, had given him permission to marry Catherine anyway. But what if the old man had been wrong?

If the new Pope, Clement VII, overturned the decision, everything would change. Henry would no longer be married. Catherine could go off and be a nun. He would be free to marry his darling Anne, and she would give him lots of sons, and they would live happily ever after.

That was how Henry saw it, anyway.

One day, chatting with his friend Thomas More, Henry abruptly raised the subject of his marriage. He was convinced, he said, that it was not just against 'the written law of God', but also 'against the law of nature'.

To More's growing discomfort, Henry took out a Bible and found the relevant page. Here, he said triumphantly. Couldn't More see it? Wasn't it obvious?

More was not so sure. He pointed out that another passage in the Bible clearly supported the marriage, and that it was unlikely the Pope would overturn his predecessor's verdict.

But Henry was deaf to reason. Later, people said he was bewitched. Some saw Anne as a sorceress, with Henry as her puppet. But there was more to it than that.

In Henry's head, his frustration at his lack of a son, his fear for the future of the Tudor dynasty, his boredom with his Spanish wife and his passion for his dark-eyed Anne were all tangled up. And by the beginning of May 1527 he had reached a decision.

He wanted a divorce. And he was going to get one, whatever the cost.

Henry knew it would not be easy. But in Cardinal Wolsey, he believed he had the perfect man for the job.

Right from the start, however, Wolsey was worried. When Henry called him into his private chamber and revealed his plans, the cardinal fell to his knees and begged his master to think again.

Grimly Henry shook his head. As Wolsey later told his servant, the King would rather put 'one half of his realm in danger' than retreat from 'any part of his will and appetite'.

So Wolsey had to come up with a solution – and quickly.

On 17 May he summoned his allies to York Place and opened an official investigation into the king's marriage. For the time being, though, the whole thing was top secret.

Wolsey's plan was to get all England's bishops to condemn the marriage. Once they presented their findings to the world, the Pope would fall into line and Catherine would have no choice but to go away.

But after only a few hours, the plan began to unravel. Wolsey was not alone in having spies at court, and by the next day Catherine's informants had told her exactly what had happened at York Place.

A lesser woman might have buckled under the shock. But Catherine thought fast.

That very day, she sent a message to the Spanish ambassador. The ambassador immediately wrote to her nephew, the Holy Roman Emperor Charles V, with the sensational news that Henry was plotting against his own wife. The Queen, he added, was 'so fearful that she dare not speak to me about it'.

For the next few weeks Henry dithered. But on 22 June, he screwed up his courage and decided to have it out with Catherine in her private chambers.

Adopting what he imagined to be a kindly tone, he explained that they had been 'in mortal sin during all the years they had lived together'. So the best thing was to separate, and for Catherine to 'choose the place to which she would retire'.

At that, Catherine burst into floods of tears. Meanwhile, Henry just stood there awkwardly, unsure what to do with himself. In the end, he mumbled something about working things out 'for the best', before slipping shamefacedly out of the door, leaving his wife sobbing behind him.

Even Henry now had to face the fact that Catherine would not go down without a fight. All her life she had battled against the turns of fate. Now, once again, God was testing her, using Anne Boleyn as his instrument.

But Catherine would meet the challenge. She would never, ever give in.

Now she raised the stakes. A few weeks later, one of her servants boarded a ship to Spain, carrying a handwritten letter to the Emperor. As soon as Charles read it, he sprang into action.

Shocked to hear of 'a case so scandalous', he wrote to Henry, insisting that he reconsider. Even more importantly, he wrote to Pope Clement VII, urging him to look into this 'ugly affair'.

From Henry's point of view, this was a disaster. Not only was the Emperor the most powerful man in Europe, but the Pope was bound to do whatever Charles told him.

A couple of months earlier, imperial mercenaries had smashed their way into Rome, rampaging through the streets, looting and killing without mercy. The Pope had fled through a secret tunnel to the Castle of the Holy Angel, where he was now a prisoner of Charles's troops.

The last thing the Pope wanted to do was to enrage the Emperor. On the other hand, he had no desire to annoy the English king, either. So he took the only obvious path. He did nothing.

The weeks went by, and Henry seethed with frustration. The summer faded. Autumn came, then winter.

On New Year's Day, Anne gave him a jewelled ship, set with a 'handsome diamond', as a token of her love. In return, Henry promised that his heart 'will be dedicated to you alone'. Every day, he assured her, he prayed to God for a divorce.

But the days passed, and nothing changed. And then, at last, Pope Clement made up his mind.

He appointed a special commission to look into the whole business. It would be held in England, with Wolsey as one of the judges. But Clement was also sending the elderly cardinal Lorenzo Campeggio, to ensure Catherine got a fair hearing.

Now there was another long delay. Aged and sickly, Campeggio did not leave Rome until August 1528, taking a ship to France. Then he had to be carried overland by litter, so he did not reach London until mid-October, six weeks after he had set out.

Almost incredibly, it was now a year and a half since Catherine had learned of Henry's plan to get rid of her. But with Campeggio's arrival, it seemed the endgame was approaching.

Anne and Henry definitely thought so. Spain's

ambassador reported that they were making plans for their wedding, since it was 'certain' Campeggio would find in their favour. But Catherine clearly had other ideas.

Soon after his arrival, the wizened old Italian came to see her and suggested that she think about retiring to a nunnery. There she would be treated with honour, while her daughter, Mary, would remain a royal princess.

Never, Catherine said. She might be a 'woman, a foreigner and friendless', but she was also a woman of honour and honesty. She was legally married, and she would never, ever say otherwise.

Even if her enemies killed her and brought her back to life, she added dramatically, she 'would prefer to die all over again, rather than change'.

At that moment, Campeggio knew there was no point in arguing. This was going to be harder than he thought.

The weeks turned into months, and still the trial did not get started. Unknown to Henry, the Pope had told Campeggio to drag the whole thing out as long as possible, and he found reason after reason to delay.

In the meantime, Henry and Catherine had no choice but to carry on living together. They spent their days in the same palaces, made public appearances in matching robes and still went to church together. They had banquets and feasts together. They watched plays together. And she even carried on sewing his shirts, as she always had.

But nobody doubted that Catherine was under dreadful strain. There was no sparkle in her tired eyes, no colour in her pale cheeks. She 'made no joy of anything', wrote one observer, 'her mind was so troubled'.

And by now, the autumn of 1528, the secret was out. In the taverns, everybody was talking about the 'King's Great Matter'. And to Henry's frustration, most of them sided with his wife.

As people said, she had done nothing wrong. Why should she suffer, just because Henry had fallen for a jumped-up nobody with a French accent?

One November morning, a crowd gathered outside Bridewell Palace, in the heart of London. They knew that every day Catherine walked along the covered bridge to the monks' chapel at nearby Blackfriars, where she liked to pray.

As soon as she came into view, people started clapping. Somebody called out, wishing her luck in the trial. Then another voice joined in; then another. Suddenly they were all shouting encouragement, urging her on and cheering for victory.

News of the incident spread fast. 'The people here are much in favour of the Queen,' the Spanish ambassador reported gleefully.

But Henry was furious. Sulking in his chamber, he ordered that in future, ordinary Londoners must be kept away from the bridge. And with his patience exhausted, he decided it was time to present his case to the great men of the kingdom.

One afternoon, Henry summoned his lords, judges and councillors to the Great Hall at Bridewell. When they were settled, he rose and began a long tirade. He wanted to explain his 'true meaning', and they must spread his message among the people.

He had nothing against Catherine. She was 'a woman of most gentleness, humility and buxomness',* and had been a most 'loving companion'. Indeed, if he had a free choice, he would still 'choose her above all other women'.

But his doubts about his marriage would not go away. 'Daily and hourly', he said, they 'trouble my conscience and vex my spirits'. He could not rest until they were addressed.

Henry sounded sincere. But his listeners knew he was not telling the whole truth. For he had never once mentioned the woman many blamed for the whole business: Anne.

The atmosphere was very 'strange', wrote one observer. Some people 'sighed and said nothing', but others were clearly 'deeply sorrowed'.

And now there came a revealing glimpse of another Henry, behind the mask of courtesy: an angry, impatient man, burning to lash out in frustration.

If anybody dared speak against him, Henry said, his tone suddenly threatening, then 'he would let him know who was master'.

---

* Obedience.

He gazed around the room, his eyes narrow and cold. There was not one head so fine, he said grimly, that he would not hesitate to cut it off.

And as his people were about to discover, he meant every word.

7

The Trial

Blackfriars, May 1529. It had been another wretched spring, and it was chilly now in the great stone chamber. But as the workmen's footsteps echoed in the emptiness, they had no time to worry about the cold. They had a job to do.

At long last, after eight months of delays, Cardinal Campeggio was ready. The date had been set for the trial of King Henry and Queen Catherine, and it was the workmen's job to prepare the stage.

The setting was the monks' upper dining hall at Blackfriars. It was a huge, bare room, but Henry wanted it to look suitably splendid.

Now the workmen moved fast. They installed the raised platform for the judges, positioning two golden chairs on richly coloured carpets. They put in benches for the spectators, and tables for the clerks.

Finally they carried in two thrones, with canopies in cloth of gold. The taller, on the right, would be Henry's. Catherine's throne went over on the left, on the other side of the spectators.

The stage was set. Everything was ready. All that was missing was the actors.

On the last day of May, resplendent in their scarlet robes, Cardinals Wolsey and Campeggio strode into the Parliament chamber. From the platform they read out the Pope's instructions, and summoned the King and Queen to appear for questioning in a few weeks' time.

Nothing like this had ever been seen in England before. Until now, nobody would have believed that the most powerful couple in the kingdom, anointed by God, could be called into open court, just like anybody else. As one of Wolsey's servants remarked, it seemed the 'strangest and newest' thing 'that ever was read or heard of in any history or chronicle'.

But this was not just the trial of the century. It would go down in history as Catherine of Aragon's finest hour.

While her husband's lawyers made their final preparations, Catherine sat with her advisers, sunk in gloom. 'She is very sad and disconsolate,' reported the Spanish ambassador, adding that she saw 'no relief from her misfortune'.

But even in the depths of her despair, Catherine had her pride. She was the daughter of Ferdinand and Isabella, a princess of Castile and Queen of England. She would not let the bullies grind her down. And when the court held its next meeting, on 18 June, she had a surprise for them.

The cardinals were about to get down to business when there was a commotion at the doorway. To gasps from the onlookers, Catherine swept into the chamber, magnificently dressed. With her came four bishops, her entire legal team and a 'great company' of ladies-in-waiting.

'Sadly and with great gravity', Catherine loudly declared that she rejected the very idea of a trial in England. Only in Rome would she get a fair hearing, and only the Pope could judge her marriage.

Clearly embarrassed, Campeggio and Wolsey played for time. Very well, they said: they would answer her objections at their next session, due to begin in three days.

That weekend, London buzzed with anticipation. And when the clerks arrived at Blackfriars on Monday, 21 June, a huge crowd was waiting outside the chamber, men and women pushing and shoving to get one of the precious places.

Shortly after nine, Catherine walked proudly into the courtroom, followed by her lawyers and ladies. A few moments later, Wolsey and Campeggio made their way through the crowd. Then, finally, in came the King.

As the crowd stood in reverence, Henry took his seat. Then Catherine moved to her throne, the cardinals took their places, and a murmur of excited anticipation rose across the hall.

'Silence!' called the court crier. 'King Harry of England, come into court!'

'Here, my lords!' said Henry, rising from his throne.

Gazing out across the chamber, his voice ringing with apparent sincerity, he began to speak. He dearly loved his wife, but he needed to know if their marriage was legal. That was the only reason they were all here. Nothing else.

Now Wolsey, sleek and well-fed, got to his feet. The Queen had questioned the fairness of the trial, but he and Campeggio were devoted to the truth. She had absolutely nothing to fear, and there was no reason for the case to go to Rome.

Now it was Catherine's turn.

'Catherine of England, come into the court!' called the crier, and a hush fell over the chamber.

Catherine rose from her seat. Silently, calmly, she pushed her way past the spectators, past the lawyers and bishops, towards her husband's gleaming throne.

And there, with deliberate suddenness, she fell to her knees. Behind her, there were loud gasps from the crowd.

Now Henry was standing. His face unreadable, he reached down and lifted his queen to her feet.

But no sooner had he done so than Catherine threw herself down again, dropping to her knees like a worshipper before her god.

'Sir,' she said huskily, her eyes on her husband, 'I beseech you for all the loves there hath been between us, and for the love of God, let me have justice.

'Take of me some pity and compassion. For I am a poor woman, a stranger . . . I have here no friend . . . I flee to you, as to the head of justice within your realm.'

A dead silence had enveloped the courtroom. The spectators, the cardinals, even Henry himself were absolutely motionless, listening to this little figure, pleading on her knees in her deep Spanish accent.

Still she was talking. How had she offended him? What had she done wrong? She had never crossed him, and had never shown 'a spark of discontent'.

'I take God and all the world,' she said, 'to witness that I have been to you a true, humble and obedient wife, ever conformable to your will and pleasure.'

For twenty years they had been husband and wife. She knew it. He knew it. 'I take God to be my judge,' she said emotionally. 'And whether it be true or no, I put it to your conscience.'

And now, gazing steadily at her husband, Catherine delivered the killer blow. Henry said he loved her. He said he wanted to know the truth about his marriage. He said he would do what God's laws decreed.

Very well. If he meant what he said, he should let her appeal to Rome, and let the Pope, the greatest churchman in the world, God's vicar on earth, deliver his verdict.

The court was absolutely silent. On his throne, Henry seemed frozen with uncertainty. All eyes were on him. There was a long, long pause.

Then, at last, he spoke. His voice was low, almost gentle. Yes, he said. Yes, she could appeal to Rome.

A shocked murmur ran around the court. Catherine rose and made a low, sweeping curtsey to her husband. Then she turned back to her seat.

But instead of resuming her place, as everybody expected, she took her lawyer's arm and kept going. Gracefully, imperiously, with the haughty elegance of a daughter of Spain, Catherine walked straight down the hall towards the door.

It was a breathtaking moment, judged to perfection. On his throne, Henry half-rose in horror, and gestured to the court crier.

'Catherine, Queen of England, come into the court!' yelled the crier.

Catherine kept walking.

'Madam, ye be called again,' muttered her lawyer.

'On, on,' Catherine said, loudly enough for people to hear. 'This is no impartial court for me, therefore I will not tarry. Go on.'

'Catherine, Queen of England!' the crier shouted again. 'Catherine, Queen of England!'

But it was too late. Catherine was gone. Behind her, on his golden chair, Henry sat as if turned to stone, his face like thunder.

The news of Catherine's dramatic performance spread quickly. Within days the Emperor's agents were working on her appeal, and by early July the imperial ambassador had delivered it to Pope Clement.

Back in London, Henry insisted that the trial must continue. In desperation, Campeggio sent a secret message to Rome, asking for orders. He could no longer drag it out, he explained, because Henry was pressing for a verdict.

The days slipped by. The moment of decision loomed ever nearer. At Blackfriars, Wolsey declared that the judges would announce their decision on Friday, 23 July.

At court, Anne Boleyn and her family no longer bothered to hide their swagger. So what if that little Spaniard had thrown a tantrum? So what if she appealed to that fool, the Pope? What good could they do?

In just a few days the court would strike down the King's marriage. Catherine would be gone, and Anne would be Queen.

Friday came. At Blackfriars, the great chamber was packed, the atmosphere electric with excitement.

Amid the hubbub, the scarlet-robed figures of Wolsey and Campeggio stepped onto the platform. High above in the gallery sat Henry, as taut and poised as a hunter, his narrow eyes fixed on the cardinals.

Then Campeggio rose from his chair, and the noise died away. The aged cardinal cleared his throat. This was it.

The court had heard all the evidence, Campeggio said, and it was clearly an important case. In fact, it was so important that he would have to discuss it in greater detail with the Pope before coming to any verdict.

A buzz went around the court – but Campeggio had not

finished. Unfortunately, he said, the papal court in Rome had just broken up for the long summer holiday. So they would take a break, too, and resume in October.

Gasps of shock echoed around the hall. On the platform, Wolsey's face was ashen.

He knew what this meant. The Pope was going to grant Catherine's appeal. The trial would move to Rome. And the King was never going to get his divorce, after all.

Some of Henry's supporters were on their feet, bellowing with rage. One of his closest friends, the Duke of Suffolk, pushed his way to the front, his face purple with anger.

So it was true what men said, Suffolk shouted, thumping the table. There never was a cardinal who did any good in England!

At that, some of the spectators glanced up at the gallery, to see what the King made of it. But the seat was empty. Henry had vanished.

With the collapse of the trial, everything changed.

Cloistered in her chamber, Anne Boleyn seethed with frustration. For three years she had waited, and still she was no closer to the prize. Someone must pay for her disappointment, and she had already selected her victim.

Anne had never liked Wolsey. He was too clever, too rich and too independent, making him a powerful rival for Henry's attention. Above all, he had been opposed to the divorce from the start.

If she and her family were to rule Henry's court, then Wolsey must be removed. And now, with the collapse of the trial, she bent her mind to his destruction.

Bringing him down would be difficult, but not impossible. After so long as Henry's right-hand man, he had made plenty of enemies.

As one writer remarked, Wolsey was 'feared by all and loved by few'. Bossy and boastful, he had made himself immensely rich. His jewels and paintings were the envy of Europe. His palaces and mansions were worthy of a king.

But now, Wolsey's enemies were muttering that he had lost his grip. To pay for Henry's wars, he had imposed heavy taxes, provoking riots across eastern England. Even abroad he seemed to have mislaid his magic touch, failing to line up a decent alliance with either the Holy Roman Empire or the French.

Now Anne saw her opportunity. Every evening she poured her poison into Henry's ear. Why hadn't Wolsey arranged the divorce? Had he really been trying? Wasn't it more likely that he had always been a traitor, working for his true master, the Pope?

Wolsey knew what Anne was doing. In private he called her the Night-Crow, scratching and pecking at his flesh. But her hold over Henry meant he was powerless to stop her.

By the late summer of 1529, Anne's allies had drawn up

a list of charges, accusing Wolsey of greed, corruption and favouring the Pope over his king. And once Campeggio had left for Italy, things began to unravel with terrifying speed.

On 9 October, Wolsey was formally charged with putting Rome's interests ahead of England's. A week later he was dismissed as Lord Chancellor.

Almost immediately, Henry's aristocratic friends, the Dukes of Norfolk and Suffolk, were hammering at the doors of York Place. Smirking with satisfaction, they ordered Wolsey to hand over the badge of his office, the Great Seal of England.

Now, with devastating suddenness, Wolsey's world fell apart. His great estates were confiscated, including his house at York Place. Already men were pulling down the silk curtains, rolling up the tapestries, piling up the treasures and heaping up the books, to carry them all off to the King.

By the time Wolsey stepped onto his river barge, still wearing his splendid crimson robes, crowds had gathered on the bank of the Thames. Most expected the boat to turn east, carrying the disgraced minister to his death at the Tower.

But at the very last moment, a horseman rode up, panting for breath and splattered with mud. It was the courtier Henry Norris, with a message from the King.

Wolsey should 'be of good cheer', Norris said, for Henry was not angry with him. The cardinal should retire to his house at Esher, Surrey. There would be no trial. If he kept his head down, Henry would protect him.

And to prove it, Norris handed over a gorgeous golden ring, as a token of Henry's friendship and support.

Wolsey fell to his knees in the mud. Tears of relief sprang to his eyes. His master was merciful, after all.

That winter, alone in a draughty, half-empty house, the exhausted Wolsey prayed to be recalled. The shock of his downfall had taken a heavy toll. His dreams were haunted by fear of the axe, and he felt so sick he struggled to breathe.

Before Christmas, Henry sent his doctor to have a look at him. Then he sent him some of his old furniture, and in February 1530 he told Wolsey he was free to take up his post as Archbishop of York.

But Anne had no intention of letting him escape so easily. All the time, her friends were whispering in the dark, spreading rumours that Wolsey was doing deals with the Pope and the French. He was plotting to block the divorce, they said, and preparing to seize power himself.

For Henry, brooding alone in his study, this was too much to bear. For years Wolsey had been his loyal servant – and more than that, his friend. And yet all the time, encouraged by Anne and her friends, his suspicions were nagging at him, like voices in the dead of night.

As month followed month, Anne wore him down. At last, on 1 November, he ordered that Wolsey be arrested and brought to London to face trial for high treason.

Five days later, beneath the black rainclouds of autumn, the cardinal bade farewell to his servants in York and prepared to ride south. His servants were in tears; they knew they would never see him again.

For almost three weeks Wolsey rode south under guard, his heavy frame shivering, his brow bright with sweat. Plagued with stomach pains, he ate little and kept nothing down. He seemed stricken with grief, a broken man, his life-force draining away.

Late on 26 November, so weak he could barely hold himself up in the saddle, Wolsey reached Leicester Abbey. Outside, in the driving rain, the monks were waiting, their torches flickering in the darkness.

'Father Abbot,' Wolsey said faintly, 'I am come hither to lay my bones among you.'

His guards helped him to his bedchamber, where for two days he lay in sweat-sodden agony. It was obvious now that the end was near.

Early on the morning of 29 November, the cardinal made his final confession. 'If I had served God as diligently as I have done the King,' he whispered hoarsely, 'he would not have given me over in my grey hairs.'

Then his words faltered, and his eyes dulled, and his breath faded to nothingness. He was dead.

In the capital, Anne and her friends greeted the news of Wolsey's death with triumphant glee.

At a dinner for the French ambassador, Anne's father, Sir Thomas Boleyn, arranged a little play to celebrate the cardinal's demise. One actor, dressed in rich red robes, played the dead man. Another played the Devil, tormenting him in the fires of hell. And all the time the Boleyns shrieked with laughter, like jackals at the feast.

Not everybody found Wolsey's death so amusing, though.

In the midst of his fall, one of his servants had come across a stocky man leaning by the window in the Great Hall at Esher, a prayer book in his hand, tears streaming down his cheeks. The man was a lawyer, and one of Wolsey's most faithful supporters. His name was Thomas Cromwell.

Cromwell was a tough, decisive man, with a reputation for getting things done. But now he wept without shame for his fallen master, and the end of all they had worked for together.

Finally, Cromwell closed the prayer book and pulled himself together. Well, there was no point in sobbing all day. He had already decided what to do. He would ride to London and get himself elected to Parliament.

And one day, long after the cardinal was buried, Thomas Cromwell would have his revenge on Anne Boleyn.

8

The Burning Begins

In the autumn of 1529, a mournful quiet fell over York Place. In the vaulted chambers where Cardinal Wolsey had managed the affairs of the nation, there came only faint rumours of the world outside.

In the chapel, the gallery, the wine cellars and kitchens, dust gathered in the shadowed corners. And in the Great Hall, once filled with the laughter of the ladies of the Green Castle, there was now only silence.

One morning, footsteps echoed on the stairs leading up from the river. Then the double doors swung open, and in walked Anne Boleyn.

Wolsey's conqueror had come to claim her spoils. And as Anne took in the rolls of tapestries and piles of precious metal plates, goblets and trinkets, a smile spread over her narrow features. The cardinal's mansion would suit her perfectly.

That Christmas, she and Henry jotted down ideas for improvements. Once they were married, York Place would be their luxury estate on the edge of London.

They would keep Wolsey's Great Hall and his soaring chapel, but they would need imposing new galleries and intimate new chambers. There would be a new park where they could stroll and ride. And there must be a new gatehouse looking out towards Westminster Abbey, so Anne and her ladies could watch the processions.

Henry would need a tiltyard, so he could practise his jousting, and a cockpit, so he could watch birds pecking each other to death. And, of course, he would want a tennis court. But would one tennis court be enough? Three tennis courts – that was more like it!

This new pleasure palace would be astonishingly expensive. But Henry was desperate to proclaim his magnificence to the world; and it was no more, he thought, than Anne deserved.

Work on the new complex, nicknamed 'Whitehall', began almost immediately.* Every morning, as builders, plasterers, painters and decorators wiped the sweat from their brows, clouds of dust from their labours rose beside the Thames.

Whitehall would become a maze of chambers and corridors, a labyrinth of winding stairs and secret corners. Never had England seen such an extravagant project. In just one year, Henry blew the equivalent of £50 million today. As

---

* The palace of Whitehall stood until 1698, when it burned down. It gave its name to the nearby street, which is still lined with government buildings today.

some men muttered, that was an awful lot of money just 'to please the lady'.

For those who dreamed of winning power at court, Wolsey's fall was a terrible warning. The closer you flew to the sun, the greater the risk of crashing to your death.

But that was the game. The court was a maze of secrets, a labyrinth of lies. It was a world of half-heard conversations and whispered conspiracies, of the silken arts of flattery and betrayal.

As Wolsey had found, success was dangerous. The further you climbed, the more enemies you made. And if you suddenly lost favour, and found yourself on the wrong side of the King, death was a real possibility.

For a man of ambition, though, the lure of power and fame was impossible to ignore. So when, in October 1529, Henry asked Sir Thomas More to succeed Wolsey as Lord Chancellor, he did not hesitate to say yes.

Now aged fifty-one, More was in the prime of life. His writings had made him famous across Europe, especially his book *Utopia*, which imagined a fantastic island with a perfect government, shared property, free hospitals and a choice of different religions.

To his friends, More's wit and learning made him one of the most admirable men alive. But there was a darker side to the man who had poured out such venom against Martin Luther and William Tyndale, and had called for Protestants to be burned in public.

Beneath the surface, More seethed with religious intensity. To punish himself for his sins, he wore a coarse hair-shirt under his expensive clothes and regularly whipped himself in the privacy of his chamber. To his friends, he was charm itself. But to people who disagreed with him, he seemed the very soul of cruelty.

Henry knew More was opposed to his divorce, but was convinced his clever friend was the right man to succeed Wolsey. So Henry promised that More would never be forced to go against his principles. He would get other people to sort out his divorce, leaving More to get on with his duties as Lord Chancellor.

More took the job. And from his very first day, he knew exactly what he wanted to do. He wanted to burn every trace of Protestantism right out of England, now and for ever.

Although the vast majority of people were still Catholics, More could feel the ground shifting beneath his feet. Thanks to the growing number of printing presses, the ideas of Luther and Tyndale were spreading more quickly than ever. People had a fresh thirst for knowledge, a new enthusiasm for argument.

This was what made the King's Great Matter so damaging. Up and down the country, people were reading about it and discussing it among themselves, some siding with Henry, others with the Pope. And instead of meekly following the great and the good, they were coming up with their own opinions.

For the new Lord Chancellor, nothing could be more dangerous. Even 'good Catholic folk', he wrote bitterly, now allowed heretics 'to talk unchecked'. There were Protestants 'in every ale house, in every tavern, in every barge, and almost every boat'; and they must be stopped.

Soon after taking office, More ordered all state officials to find and destroy these 'malicious and wicked' rebels. All Tyndale's works, including the Bible, were forbidden by law, and anybody caught with them would be arrested.

More led some police missions personally, bursting into suspected heretics' homes, scouring their shelves and dragging them off to the cells if they had the wrong books. He led armed men to smash printing presses, and had heretics paraded through the streets before a jeering mob.

Rumour had it that he had some Protestants brought to his house and whipped in front of him, his eyes glittering with fanatical cruelty. And some witnesses reported that More had personally tortured prisoners in the Tower of London, stretching them on the rack until their joints popped and their bones cracked.

The first burning came within weeks. At the end of 1529 a Norfolk priest called Thomas Hitton had been caught with smuggled letters from the Protestant exiles sewn into his coat.

More called him 'the Devil's stinking martyr' and ordered that he be questioned under torture. When Hitton confessed that he doubted the miracle of the Mass, his fate was sealed.

On 23 February 1530, Hitton was burned at the stake, the first English Protestant to die for his beliefs. Others soon followed.

Another priest, Thomas Bilney, was burned for doubting the powers of the saints. Richard Bayfield was burned for owning forbidden books, while James Bainham was burned for declaring that Purgatory was a fraud.

Burning was a dreadful death: spectacular, slow and horrifically painful. If the wind was blowing the wrong way, it could take hours for people to die, roasted as the spectators looked on.

Yet More's victims died with astonishing courage. As James Bainham was led to his death, he shouted: 'I die for having said it is lawful for every man and woman to have God's book!' And as his body began to smoulder, he had the strength to call out: 'The Lord forgive Sir Thomas More!'

But they were the last words he ever said.

If the scales had tipped another way, perhaps More's blood-thirsty tactics would have worked. Perhaps he would have bullied the doubters into sullen silence. Perhaps the Protestant cause would have perished in his fires, and England would have remained loyal to Rome.

But it was at this moment, when her country's future hung in the balance, that Anne Boleyn made her mark on history.

Anne had always been interested in new ideas. As a teenager in Paris she had read French versions of the Bible, as well as books discussing the future of the Church.

Back in London, she became a familiar face at the capital's bookshops, quietly buying some of the more daring titles. And since she was so close to the King, she was able to protect some of her favourite writers and booksellers from the authorities.

But now she went further. With the Pope apparently determined to block Henry's divorce, she saw a chance to win two battles at once, clearing a path to her marriage and promoting the Protestant cause in England.

In private, Anne showed Henry some of the books she had collected. One was a pamphlet by Tyndale's friend Simon Fish, who had accused Catholic priests of being greedy and corrupt, and urged the King to take over the powers of the Church.

Then, in the autumn of 1529, Anne showed the King an even more dangerous book: Tyndale's *The Obedience of a Christian Man*. As a renegade wanted for heresy, Tyndale was still in exile. But Anne knew some of his ideas would appeal to Henry, and she had marked the crucial passages for him by scratching the pages with her fingernail.

Tyndale claimed that the Catholic Church had been plotting against England for centuries. Throughout history, the popes had lied and cheated to increase their own power, inventing fake relics and murdering anybody who stood in their way.

In reality, Tyndale said, the 'Antichrist of Rome' had no right to wield any power in England. It was the King who should lead the English Church. For 'God hath made the King in every realm judge over all, and over him there is no judge'.

Henry had always thought of himself as a good Catholic. But as he read those words, his eyes widened. This, he said excitedly, was a book 'for me and all kings to read'.

Step by step, Anne was coaxing Henry away from Rome. Over the next few months, his servants pored through the history books, looking for evidence to support his case. And by the late summer of 1530, they had put together a dossier 'proving' that the Pope was merely the Bishop of Rome, with no power in England.

Henry loved it. By now, he was persuaded that England was not just another European kingdom, but an independent empire in its own right. And he was not just its king. He was Supreme Head of the Church, 'God's Vicar on Earth', 'Emperor and Pope in his own kingdom'.

To some people, this seemed unimaginably shocking. The Pope was the head of Western Christendom, and England's kings had knelt before him for as long as anybody could remember.

But the long saga of the divorce had damaged Henry's pride. Humiliated in public, he had been seething for months. Now he itched to lash out in revenge.

And when the Pope's ambassador warned that he was in danger of being kicked out of the Catholic Church, Henry lost his temper.

'Let the Pope do what he will!' he shouted. 'I care not a fig . . . Let him follow his own way at Rome. I will do here what I think best!'

As Henry ranted and raved, Anne seemed haughtier than ever. To many people, she now behaved as if she was Queen already.

She treated Catherine's ladies-in-waiting with cold contempt, remarking that she wished 'all the Spaniards in the world would drown in the sea'. When one of them complained, Anne snapped that 'she cared not for the Queen or any of her family', and would happily see Catherine hanged.

For Catherine, life had become a series of daily humiliations. In May 1531 her husband sent a small army of noblemen and bishops, led by the Dukes of Norfolk and Suffolk, to confront her at Greenwich and frighten her into surrender.

But when they urged her to withdraw her appeal to Rome, Catherine shook her head. No, she said. All she wanted was justice, and if they had 'experienced one half of the hard days and nights' she had suffered, they would want the same.

Once again Catherine had been cast as the lone heroine, standing up to the most powerful men in the land. Deep down, many of Henry's men admired her for it, but they never dared to tell him that.

By now the atmosphere at court was stiflingly tense, and many people were relieved when the whole crew – Henry and Anne, Catherine and her daughter Mary, and all their attendants, courtiers and hangers-on – decamped to Windsor for the summer. But even here, at the King's country retreat, there was no escape from the black looks and muttered asides.

Then, on the morning of 14 July, Catherine awoke to find the royal apartments deserted. An attendant nervously explained that Henry had risen early to go on a hunting trip – and had taken the Lady Anne with him.

Though Catherine did not at first realize it, this was the final breach. Her husband was gone. She would never see him again.

After a day or two, Catherine sent a messenger with a note. She hoped her husband was well, and was sorry to have missed him before he left. It would be nice, she added with cool politeness, if she could have a chance to say goodbye.

Perhaps because the letter pricked his conscience, Henry

was furious. 'He cared not for her farewells', he told the messenger, and 'had no wish to offer her the consolation of which she spoke or any other'. He wanted 'no more of her messages'. In fact, he just wanted her gone.

On Catherine, her husband's harsh words fell like a hammer-blow. But there was worse to follow. A few days later, another message arrived from the King. His trip was almost over, and he was coming back to Windsor with the Lady Anne.

So Catherine must clear out, right away. He had arranged for her to stay at one of Wolsey's old country houses, The More, in Hertfordshire.* Under no circumstances, though, could she take Mary with her. The teenage princess would be escorted to the royal palace at Richmond.

For Catherine, the wheel of fortune had taken many cruel turns, but this was the cruellest yet. She had given the best years of her life to Henry and to England. But now, after more than two decades of marriage, she had been cast aside like an old rag doll.

Her husband had not even had the decency to say good-bye. And to cap it all, her beloved daughter was being taken away. Now, more than ever, she was on her own.

---

* The More had nothing to do with Thomas More.

In the autumn of 1531, as the evenings drew in and the gold faded in the trees, a sad, grey figure wandered alone in the gardens of The More.

The estate had been one of Wolsey's finest, famed across Europe for its splendid deer park. But already the buildings were looking tired, the gardens ragged and overgrown.

Although Catherine kept her servants, she felt like a prisoner. Few visitors were allowed in to see her, and she told the imperial ambassador that she would rather be locked up in the Tower of London. At least then the world would know how badly she was treated.

Yet still this stubborn little figure remained defiant. She was still married; she was still Queen. They could punish her, imprison her, even torture her. But she would die before she denied the truth.

Christmas came: the loneliest, saddest time of all. It was months since she had seen Mary.

For the first time since her wedding day, there was no present from Henry. Catherine did not even get any gifts from the gentlemen of the court, because her husband had banned them from contacting her.

At court, too, the mood was gloomy. 'All men said there was no mirth in that Christmas,' wrote one chronicler, 'because the Queen and the ladies were absent.'

Tired after the months of arguing, Henry was in no mood to celebrate. When Catherine sent him a golden cup to mark the New Year, he exploded. He wanted nothing to do with her, he said. Get rid of it!

The year 1532 opened, cheerless and cold. As always, it rained. Winds battered the coast of England.

There was a threat in the air: a kind of restlessness, a sense of looming violence. In the eastern counties there were reports of attacks on shrines and statues. In the village of Dovercourt, Essex, three men were hanged for burning the church's huge wooden cross, which had attracted pilgrims for years.

Brooding in his study, Thomas More was adamant that there must be no let-up in the war against the heretics. Just two weeks into the New Year his latest victim was burned before a crowd in Exeter.

Thomas Benet was a quiet, serious man, who had always kept himself to himself. He was a teacher who had moved to Devon with his young family because he thought it would be safer to follow his Protestant principles there, far from the capital.

But in the autumn of 1531 he had been caught putting up posters on the church door which read: 'The Pope is Antichrist; and we ought to worship God only, and no saints.'

Arrested and interrogated, Benet refused to break. He 'would do it again', he said; for he had written 'nothing but the very truth'.

Even as his captors lit the bonfire, Benet did not falter. 'Father, forgive them,' he said calmly. Then the flames flickered higher, and he spoke no more.

That same day in London, Parliament met after the

Christmas break. The subject on everybody's minds was the same as ever: the King's divorce.

But Henry had run out of patience. Anne had worn him down at last. He had decided, once and for all, to break with Rome.

PART TWO

ANNE BOLEYN

9

Anne the Queen

Easter Sunday, 1532. In every village in England, families had gathered to celebrate new life and new hope, the resurrection of Jesus and the coming of spring.

For young and old alike, it was one of the highlights of the year: a day of rich roast lamb and sweet Easter buns. And at Greenwich Palace, where Henry and Anne led their courtiers to the Easter Mass, everybody was looking forward to wine and laughter.

But William Peto, the friar preaching that day's sermon, had other ideas.

When Peto climbed into the pulpit, nobody had any inkling of what he was going to say. But as his voice echoed around the church, his listeners soon realized that this was not a typical Easter sermon.

Fixing his eyes on the King, Peto began with a Bible story: the tale of King Ahab. Bewitched by the wicked Jezebel, Ahab led his people to disaster. And the couple, too, came to terrible ends.

Shot by an archer, Ahab died in an undignified heap,

while dogs licked up his blood. As for Jezebel, she was thrown from a window and trampled by horses, before the dogs were let loose to feast on her flesh.

Here, said Peto, was a lesson for Henry. He was in danger of becoming England's Ahab. If he persisted with this plan to divorce his wife, he would come to the same 'unhappy end', and the dogs would 'lick your blood as they did his'.

After the service, Henry went straight up to the friar, his face purple with fury at this extraordinary insolence. But Peto showed not a flicker of fear. If the King 'did not take care', he said coolly, 'he would be in great danger of losing his kingdom', since 'all his subjects, high and low,' were completely opposed to his divorce.

Henry stormed out of the chapel. A few days later, he ordered Peto's arrest, and for the rest of the year the friar lingered in prison.

But to some of the King's friends, this was a sign that his obsession with Anne Boleyn was dragging him into dangerous waters.

From almost every part of the country there were reports of unrest, of preachers being heckled and shouted down. In every tavern and marketplace in England, people grumbled that the King had lost his head, bewitched by that jumped-up little minx, 'Nan Bullen'. And as week followed week, the temperature was rising.

The saga of the Great Matter had been going on for almost six years, and Henry desperately needed a solution. But one man's crisis was another's opportunity. And as Henry seethed, Cardinal Wolsey's old right-hand man was plotting a route out of the maze.

It was more than two years since Thomas Cromwell had wept at his master's fall. But now, with Henry's kingdom in turmoil, this cool, calculating man saw his chance to stamp his vision on England's history.

There was something mysterious, something endlessly unknowable, about Thomas Cromwell. Stocky and thick-set, he was a man of secrets. Nobody was ever quite sure who he was or what he wanted.

Like his friend Wolsey, Cromwell had pulled himself up from nothing. He came from Putney, a village near London, where his father brewed beer and was often in trouble for fighting.

As a young man he had left to pursue his destiny abroad. He had served as a soldier of fortune in Italy, worked for a rich Florentine banker and spent time trading cloth in the Low Countries.

So went the rumours, anyway. Nobody was ever really certain, and Cromwell never cared to give the details.

Back in London he worked for Wolsey and was elected to Parliament. He was clever, tireless and completely reliable. He knew how things worked, what strings to pull and which arms to twist. And to Henry, that made him the perfect servant.

But there was something Cromwell did not tell his master. In secret, he was a committed Protestant. Thanks to his Continental contacts, he had almost certainly read Tyndale's Bible – although Cromwell being Cromwell, nobody could be quite sure.

That meant he was playing a double game. Deep down he despised Anne Boleyn, whom he had never forgiven for the death of Wolsey.

But his revenge could wait. In the meantime, he planned to use Anne, and the whole business of the divorce, to promote the cause of Protestantism in England.

Quietly, steadily, Cromwell worked on the King, suggesting that there was a neat, simple solution to the whole mess.

If Henry broke the link with Rome, he wouldn't just get his divorce. He would be master in his own kingdom, free to take over the Church's lands and become the richest king England had ever seen.

To some of Henry's councillors, Cromwell's vision of unchecked royal power was positively chilling. Thomas More begged him to tell the King 'what he *ought* to do but never what he is *able* to do'. For if the 'lion knew his own strength', it would be impossible for other men to control him.

But as Cromwell's star rose, More's was falling. The King was fickle: one moment you had his favour, the next you were out.

By the spring of 1532, Cromwell had prepared the ground. And on 11 May, a few weeks after that Easter sermon, Henry announced that his churchmen must choose. Were they loyal to England, or to Rome?

Four days later, he sent his councillors to bully the bishops. They must give up their power to make their own rules and run their own affairs. That power now belonged to him.

For the best part of a day the bishops hesitated. But many felt they had little choice. And so, the following afternoon, they gave Henry what he wanted: the complete surrender of the English Church.

It was, in its way, a revolution. No major European country had ever done anything like it. No English king had ever wielded such unfettered power. And never had the Catholic Church been brought so low.

For Thomas More, it was too much to bear. That afternoon, in the garden of Whitehall, he handed the King a leather pouch containing the Great Seal of England. He could no longer carry on as Lord Chancellor, he said.

For weeks More had been wrestling with his conscience. A man of enormous ambition, he hated the thought of resigning. But as a loyal servant of the Catholic Church, he could not be part of a regime dismantling its power and privileges.

As he said farewell to his old master, More promised not to cause trouble. He would retire to his library, and 'never again study or meddle with any matter of this world'.

Henry nodded. He quite understood. He would never

put More 'in trouble of his conscience'. He would always be a 'good and gracious lord'.

But as More walked away, his head bowed, he knew Henry had made such promises before.

After all, Cardinal Wolsey had been his right-hand man. And Catherine of Aragon had been his wife, his queen and the mother of his daughter.

And More knew only too well what had happened to them . . .

With More gone, nobody stood between the Boleyn family and the prize they had sought for so long.

That autumn, Henry and Anne sailed for France aboard the ship *Swallow*. Henry was hoping to agree a new treaty with King Francis, and this time he wanted Anne to be centre stage.

Anne had packed her finest gowns, as well as the jewels her husband had reclaimed from the despairing Catherine.

When they arrived in Calais, King Francis sent her a huge diamond as a welcome present. Then, after he had joined them for dinner, it was time for dancing.

Anne led the group of seven masked ladies, and Francis

led the seven men. Afterwards, the two of them withdrew to a quiet corner, chatting for a while in French.

For Anne, it was a moment of sweet victory. Her days of skulking in the background were over. In the eyes of the world, she was the first lady of England.

Meanwhile, Henry was laying the foundations for the next step. The old Archbishop of Canterbury had died at the end of August, and it was his job to name a replacement.

Henry soon made up his mind. In late October, he ordered his ambassador at the imperial court, a young churchman called Thomas Cranmer, to come home at once.

Cranmer was by no means the most obvious candidate. But Henry could trust him. A few years earlier Cranmer had helped to muster support for the King's divorce, and he had also put together the dossier arguing that the King should be in charge of the English Church. Above all, the Boleyns thought very highly of him.

Unlike most of Henry's other advisers, Cranmer was not greedy for power. He was a modest, unassuming, kind-hearted man.

But like Thomas Cromwell, Cranmer had a secret. While travelling abroad, he had become keenly interested in Protestant ideas. In Germany he had even secretly got married, an extraordinarily dangerous step for a priest.

Not surprisingly, Cranmer did not breathe a word of this to Henry. Instead, he made his way home, taking up his new duties at the beginning of 1533.

Now everything was in place. Wolsey was dead, More

was gone, Cromwell controlled Parliament and Cranmer was running the Church. And the bonds between England and Rome had frayed almost to nothingness.

Late in the afternoon of 24 January, Henry slipped away from Greenwich Palace and ordered his barge to head for Whitehall. Early the following morning, in a chamber above the magnificent new gatehouse, Anne and Henry were married by one of Wolsey's old priests.

After the years of waiting, it was a strangely low-key occasion. There were just two witnesses: the King's groom and Anne's lady-in-waiting. But there were no trumpeters, no heralds, no guests and no crowds.

When it was all over, Henry quietly returned to Greenwich. He had kept his promise. Anne was his wife.

It was just a shame he had a wife already.

For the people of England, these were strange and un-settling times. Things they had taken for granted all their lives were being turned on their heads.

In churches across the land, Protestant preachers now went further than ever. People were wrong, they said, to worship the Virgin Mary, wrong to kneel before the saints and wrong to believe in the power of relics. As for

Purgatory, it was a colossal con, designed to line the pockets of the Pope and his priests.

Many ordinary people no longer knew what, or whom, to believe. Forbidden ideas were now being openly discussed. Yet at the same time, traditions celebrated for centuries, such as relics and pilgrimages, were being held up for savage mockery.

In the alehouses, men muttered that this was all King Henry's fault. It had all started when he had taken up with that witch Nan Bullen. Now he wanted people to read the Bible in English!

As the arguments raged, Cromwell was preparing the next step in his quiet revolution.

For months he had been working on a new law to smash the link with Rome for ever. In the spring of 1533 he unveiled it to the House of Commons.

The title, 'An Act in Restraint of Appeals', made it sound a bit dull, but it was not dull at all. In effect, it was England's Declaration of Independence – from the previously all-powerful Catholic Church.

'This realm of England,' the text declared grandly, 'is an Empire . . . governed by one Supreme Head and King.' God had given the King 'whole and entire power', and no foreign prince or priest could do anything about it.

So, from now on, the Act said, it was illegal for people to go crying to the 'Bishop of Rome'. The Pope had no sway in England. His laws were not welcome. His opinions were not wanted.

For some of England's MPs, born and bred as devout

Catholics, this was going too far. But in his watchful way, Cromwell was utterly ruthless. After calling in one wavering MP, Sir George Throckmorton, he sternly advised him to 'stay at home and meddle little in politics'.

Throckmorton got the message. In the first week of April, the new Act became law.

A few days later, riders arrived at Ampthill Castle in Bedfordshire. This was Catherine of Aragon's latest gilded cage, where she was kept in captivity, abandoned by her husband and cut off from her daughter.

Led by the Duke of Suffolk, the visitors brought a message from the King. Henry had finally summoned the courage to tell his wife that he had married somebody else. And to rub salt into the wound, Anne was now expecting a child.

For Catherine, this was the latest in a series of shattering blows. But there were no tears, no tantrums. She stiffened her jaw and nodded silently, as she always did.

Then, two months later, came perhaps the greatest blow of all.

On Sunday, 1 June 1533, Anne Boleyn reached the summit of all her desires, and was crowned Queen of England in Westminster Abbey.

As for his and Catherine's coronation all those years ago, Henry spared no expense. His new queen arrived in London by boat, dressed in cloth of gold and escorted by fifty barges of smiling minstrels. At the Tower of London, the cannons fired so many salutes that, according to one observer, it seemed 'as if all the houses must tumble to the ground'.

The day before her coronation, Anne paraded through

the City, just like Catherine before her. She wore a velvet gown, glittering with pearls and diamonds. Her thick black hair flowed down her back, and in her hand she carried a bunch of flowers.

Once again the streets were decorated with pageants. At St Paul's, where she was greeted by maidens, a banner read in Latin: 'Queen Anne, when thou shalt bear a new son of the King's blood, there shall be a golden world unto thy people.'

A son. That was what this whole business had always been about.

There were crowds, of course. London loved a show. But they showed little enthusiasm for the King's new bride.

Few people raised their caps, and even fewer shouted 'God save the Queen!' And Anne noticed. When it was all over, and her husband took her in his arms, it was the first thing she said.

Perhaps it was then that Anne realized the truth. She had taken Catherine's husband, her throne, even her jewels. But she would never take her rival's place in the hearts of the people.

A month later, gazing out from her window at Ampthill, Catherine saw horsemen in the distance.

Once again, they came with a message from Henry. Her marriage had been proclaimed 'detestable, abominable . . . and directly against the laws of God and nature'. And as a result, she was no longer entitled to call herself Queen.

Catherine's eyes narrowed. She was visibly older now, pale and tired, her face etched with anxiety, her short body racked by a painful cough. But she had not changed.

She was still Queen, she said coldly. Her husband would never break her.

When the riders reported back, Cromwell gave a wry smile. God had wronged Catherine, he said quietly, 'in not making her a man'. She was so brave, so determined, that 'she would have surpassed in glory and fame' the greatest princes of the world.

Even if Catherine had heard them, Cromwell's words would have brought little consolation. That summer, Henry ordered her to move to the Bishop of Lincoln's house at Buckden, a day's ride away. As she was no longer a queen, she must live more simply from now on.

But as Catherine mounted her horse, something extraordinary happened.

Waiting along the lane, the villagers had come to say goodbye. Many of them cheered and clapped; others had tears running down their cheeks.

Although people were forbidden on pain of death from calling her the Queen, many of them did it anyway, shouting it out at the tops of their voices. They lined the road all the way to Buckden – a welcome reminder that her adopted people had not forgotten her.

Eventually, the bishop's house came into view. Catherine dismounted and stepped inside. The door swung shut, and all was silent.

A few weeks later, at the end of August, Anne withdrew to her chamber to prepare for the coming of her baby. The court was electric with excitement. All the doctors and astrologers were agreed: it would be a boy.

Here, after all these years, was the moment about which Henry had dreamed. Everything was ready, down to the arrangements for the great celebratory tournament. The only question was whether the little boy would be called Henry or Edward.

On the afternoon of 7 September, the baby came.

Everything went perfectly. Anne was in good health, and the baby could not have been prettier. There was only one slight problem.

It was a girl.

10

Behold the Head of a Traitor!

Elizabeth Barton was only a teenager when she had her first vision.

Born in the Kentish countryside, unable to read or write, Elizabeth worked as a servant. A serious, anxious girl, she ate very little and was often ill.

One day in 1525, the fit came upon her. To her fellow servants she seemed to have fallen into a trance, her body writhing, her eyes rolling, her voice babbling uncontrollably.

She saw Jesus and his mother, Mary. She saw pilgrims on earth and the saints in heaven. She saw St Michael saving the souls of the dead, and St Peter with the keys to paradise.

As her visions continued, Elizabeth's reputation spread. She became a nun, entering a convent in Canterbury. Men and women travelled from all over England to seek her advice, among them some of the most powerful people in the land.

Before his fall, Cardinal Wolsey met her several times. She had even been invited to meet King Henry, who listened with rapt fascination to her stories of seeing Jesus.

By the early 1530s, the 'Maid of Kent' was one of the best-known women in England. But now her prophecies took on a new edge.

England, she warned, was facing utter ruin. Plague, rebellion and war were at hand. And it was all because of the King's wicked scheme to get rid of his wife, break with the Pope and marry Anne Boleyn.

If Henry continued down this path, he would lose his throne. She had seen him in her dreams, dying of the plague. She had even seen the place reserved for him in hell.

This kind of talk was immensely dangerous. In private, one of her keenest admirers, Sir Thomas More, implored her to keep quiet about 'princes' affairs'.

But Elizabeth would not stop. Instead, her visions became more shocking than ever. She saw Jesus on the cross, writhing in agony because of Henry's wickedness. She saw Anne Boleyn's body being eaten by dogs. She saw the Tudors driven from power, and the Plantagenet family restored to the throne of England.

At any time, such claims would have been reckless. But in the fevered atmosphere surrounding Anne's coronation, they were suicidal.

In the summer of 1533, Barton was summoned to meet Thomas Cromwell. Coolly, methodically, he asked her question after question, probing her answers for evidence of treason.

A few weeks later she was dragged before the King's council. And finally, under relentless interrogation, she cracked. Yes, she sobbed, she was a heretic and a traitor. Yes, her visions and prophecies had been frauds all along.

On 23 November, Barton was paraded in the centre of London and forced to grovel for her sins. Beside her on the platform, one of Henry's bishops lifted his voice to the heavens, shrill with contempt for her false miracles and dishonest claims.

For Barton, it was a shattering humiliation. But when it was over, the guards did not let her go free.

Instead, they pushed her into the cart, and turned towards the Tower of London. The King had not finished with Elizabeth Barton.

For England's new Queen, life should have been perfect.

Anne Boleyn had all the dresses, jewels and finery she could have wanted. Henry had already ordered lavish decorations for her new apartments at Greenwich, Whitehall and Hampton Court. And her family had been garlanded with riches and honours.

But even at the height of her glory, the anxieties nagged away at her. Her baby daughter, Elizabeth, was perfectly healthy, but Anne had promised Henry a son, and he was not famous for his patience.

Above all, she knew the people did not like her. She had seen them standing in sullen silence during her coronation procession; and every week she heard the stories.

There was the woman in Suffolk who had called her a 'naughty, goggle-eyed' witch. There was the Lancashire vicar who said only the Devil could have made her Queen of England; there was the Warwickshire priest who called for her to be burned at the stake.

On 23 August 1533, Henry's men demonstrated the consequences of insulting his wife. That morning they dragged two women to the bustling market at Cheapside, which ran along the river.

As a crowd gathered, the women were stripped to the waist, before they were nailed by their ears to a post. This, the guards cried, was the punishment for all those who dared to gossip about England's new Queen.

But when the two women were finally released, their ears smeared with blood, they were not sorry. They would be glad to die, they said loudly, 'for Queen Catherine's sake'.

'Queen Catherine'. The two words from which Anne could never escape; the drumbeat that sounded in her head when she closed her eyes at night.

And although the former queen had been safely put away, Anne still had to face her daughter, Mary. Pale, sickly and intense, the teenage Mary had never forgiven her father for what he had done to her mother. If looks could kill, she would have murdered Anne many times over.

Just before Christmas, 1533, Mary was sent to Hatfield House in Hertfordshire, to serve her baby half-sister,

Elizabeth, as a lady-in-waiting. This, Anne thought, would teach her some humility.

But Mary had her mother's Spanish spirit. When she arrived, she stubbornly refused to refer to Elizabeth as Princess of Wales. 'That is the title that belongs to me by right, and to no one else,' she said firmly.

She even refused to eat her dinner in the same hall as the baby, because she would have to sit in an inferior place. Instead, Mary took her meals in her bedchamber, sobbing loudly behind the door.

Back in London, Anne seethed with fury. She would bring this spoiled brat to heel, if it was the last thing she ever did.

When she next went to Hatfield, she sent a note to Mary inviting her 'to visit her and honour her as Queen'. Surely, she thought, the girl would have to come out.

From behind the door of her room, Mary sent a note back. Unfortunately, she wrote, she 'knew no Queen in England' except her mother Catherine. So she would be staying in her room, thank you.

As Anne left Hatfield, her fox-like face was contorted with rage. How dare this little brat defy her? One day, she would 'bring down the pride of this unbridled Spanish blood'.

Anne did not have to wait long for her revenge. On 23 March 1534, Parliament approved a momentous new law.

Prepared by Thomas Cromwell, the Act of Succession erased Catherine and Mary from the royal family. When Henry died, England's crown would go to Anne's future son; and failing that, to the baby Elizabeth.

Under Cromwell's new law, any criticism of the King's divorce was treason, punishable by death. Even if you were chatting in the alehouse with your friends, you were risking your life just to mention it.

Most alarming of all was the oath. Under the new law, every man and woman in England was ordered to swear an oath to uphold Henry's second marriage, the succession of Anne's children and the King's position as Supreme Head of the Church.

To people in the sixteenth century, swearing an oath was an immensely solemn undertaking. If you swore falsely, you were putting your soul in terrible danger.

But if you refused to swear, the new Act had a vicious sting in the tail. Refusal was high treason. And if anybody doubted that Henry and Cromwell meant what they said, they had prepared a spectacular demonstration.

On 20 April, the day the people of London lined up to swear the new oath, Elizabeth Barton emerged from the Tower.

Pale and thin after months in prison, the Maid of Kent was strapped to a wooden frame. Tethered behind a horse, she was dragged along the muddy, filth-splattered streets towards Tyburn, beyond the city's western gates.

There, before a vast crowd, she was hanged by the neck from a gibbet. At the last minute, when she was only seconds from death, the guards cut her down and dragged her to the block.

The executioner lifted his axe; the crowd held its breath . . .

A few hours later, Elizabeth Barton's severed head was staring down at the people of London from a pike above London Bridge. As it happened, that was the very spot where Catherine of Aragon had first ridden into the city, all those years ago.

That summer, in every village in England, men and women lined up to swear the oath. With Barton's fate so fresh in their minds, hardly any of them refused.

But one man said no.

Thomas More knew the risks of disobedience better than anybody. As Lord Chancellor he had condemned many heretics to the flames, and he did not regret it.

Yet not only was More totally opposed to the King's divorce, he was passionately devoted to the Catholic Church. And as he read the words of the oath, he shook his head.

As he explained to Henry's officers, his conscience would not let him do it. If he swore, he would be sending his 'soul to eternal damnation'.

More and Henry were old friends. But even with his friends, Henry always had to get his way. Defiance meant opposition. Opposition meant treason. And treason meant death.

On 17 April, More was sent to the Tower of London. He was allowed books and pens, and his family could visit him. But he would never set foot outside again as a free man.

Spring gave way to summer. Outside, the people of London enjoyed the sunshine. But in his dank stone cell, More scribbled quietly away, still refusing to budge.

The skies darkened, the evenings lengthened and autumn came. In November, Parliament approved more steps towards Cromwell's new England.

The Act of Supremacy confirmed that the King was now 'Supreme Head on Earth of the Church of England', controlling all its wealth, income and power.

Meanwhile the Treasons Act made it illegal to 'wish, will or desire' any harm to Henry, Anne or Elizabeth. Even to 'imagine' harm to them was treason, and it was also treason to call the King a heretic or a tyrant. The penalty was death.

Never before had a king tried to control people's words, let alone their thoughts. But there had never been a king like Henry: so moody, so suspicious, so *dangerous*.

To ordinary people, it was as if England had been convulsed by an earthquake, turning all the old ideas on their heads. And with things changing so fast, it was now risky to voice any opinion at all.

In the meantime, Cromwell, the brewer's son from Putney, was piling up offices and titles with breathtaking speed. He was already the King's Chief Secretary and Master of the Rolls, with a magnificent house on the edge of the City.

That Christmas, Cromwell gained a new title, 'Vicar-General and Vice-Gerent in Spirituals'. In effect, he now had complete power over the Church of England. All churches and monasteries, all priests and friars, had to follow his orders.

Now Cromwell seized his chance to turn England into a citadel of the new Protestantism – by force, if necessary. Preachers were encouraged to praise the King, pour scorn on the Pope and question the rituals of the Catholic Church.

Even the English language was beginning to change. People who supported the 'Bishop of Rome' were no longer Catholics: they were 'Papists'.

Many older priests were horrified. Cromwell's new preachers 'called themselves Children of Christ', wrote one, 'but they were Children of the Devil'.

Cromwell knew the old guard were against him. But he meant to bend them to his will.

In the summer of 1535, he ordered every bishop in England to speak out in favour of the new order. Every week they must hammer home the message that Henry was Supreme Head of the Church, Catherine had never been his true wife and Elizabeth, not Mary, was the true heir. The very word 'Pope' must be scratched out of their prayer books.

Cromwell knew, though, that some bishops put their loyalty to Rome above their loyalty to England. So in secret, he also sent handwritten orders to every judge and magistrate in the country.

Any bishop or priest speaking up for the Pope must be arrested at once. He wanted regular reports with details of suspected traitors. And if any of the judges was to 'halt, stumble or wink' in his duties, he would himself be punished so severely that 'all the world besides shall take example and beware'.

Cromwell meant what he said. That summer, London's executioners were busier than ever.

A few weeks earlier, the vicar of Isleworth, John Hale, had accused the King of being a robber and a tyrant, 'puffed with vainglory and pride . . . more foul and more stinking than a sow, wallowing and defiling herself in any filthy place'.

Hale was thrown into the Tower of London, along with four monks who had refused to accept the King's supremacy over the Church. On 4 May, the five men were tied upside down on wooden frames and dragged through the rutted lanes to Tyburn.

Like Elizabeth Barton, they were hanged until they were choking for breath, before the hangman cut them down. Then, while each man was still alive, the executioner sliced them open and burned their organs in front of them.

Only then did the executioner cut each victim's head off. Finally, he sliced the bodies into four quarters, each of which was impaled on a pike as a warning to the people of London.

As usual, all this unfolded before a vast crowd. In Tudor England, this was many people's idea of a jolly family outing.

A month later, Henry put on another bloodthirsty show, involving three more monks who had refused to bow to his supremacy. To break their spirits, they had been forced to stand upright for two weeks in the Marshalsea Prison, chained at the neck and covered with their own filth. But still they refused to give in.

On 19 June, they were dragged to Tyburn. There, like their five comrades, they were hanged, tortured and beheaded. And as the sunlight began to fade, the birds were already feasting on their quartered bodies, high above the walls of the City.

From his cell in the Tower, Thomas More had watched thoughtfully as the monks were led out. The prisoners, he murmured, were going to their deaths as cheerfully 'as bridegrooms to their marriage'.

After months behind bars, More was a shadow of his former self, his hair long and grey, his face lined and haggard. He had long since lost hope of survival, and spent his time thinking and writing. But he never wavered in his refusal to swear the oath.

Twice Cromwell visited him in the Tower, promising that the King would show mercy if More changed his mind. Why wouldn't he do it? What were his reasons?

More smiled. He had promised never to 'meddle' in politics, he said, so he was not going to discuss his reasons. His conscience would not let him swear, and that was all there was to it.

On 12 June, the Solicitor General, Richard Rich, arrived to confiscate More's books – an especially cruel gesture, given how much he loved reading and writing.

Then, on 1 July, More was taken to Westminster Hall to face trial on four counts of treason. Before him sat more than a dozen judges, among them Cromwell, Anne's father and brother, and almost all the leading noblemen of the realm.

Dressed in a rough woollen gown, More was so weak that he was given special permission to sit. But he remained as obstinate as ever. He was no traitor, he said calmly, but he would not swear the oath.

Then the judges played their trump card. Stepping forward from the shadows, Richard Rich claimed that while he had been collecting the prisoner's books, More had told him that Parliament had no right to make Henry head of the Church of England.

At this, More almost laughed in disbelief. Calling God as his witness, he insisted that Rich was lying. Then he turned to the judges.

Was it plausible that 'in so weighty a cause' he would have trusted somebody like Rich, universally known as a man 'of very little truth'? 'Can this, in your judgements, my lords, seem likely to be true?'

It was no good. The jury took less than a quarter of an hour to decide their verdict: Guilty.

Now, when he had nothing to lose, More broke his silence.

He had not taken the oath, he said scornfully, because it was 'repugnant to the laws of God'. Parliament had no right to break the link with Rome, and Henry had no right to seize the powers of the Pope. They might be able to find one bishop who agreed with them. But he would be able to find a hundred who didn't.

When he had finished, the judges read the sentence: Death.

Early on the morning of 6 July, More was led onto Tower Hill. 'His beard was long,' wrote one chronicler, 'his face pale and thin, and carrying a red cross in his hand, he often lifted up his eyes to heaven.'

As More mounted the steps to the execution block, his legs buckled and for a moment he stumbled. 'Pray, sir,' he said wryly to the guard, 'see me safe up; and as to my coming down, let me shift for myself.'

He turned to the crowd. 'I die the King's good servant,' he said clearly, 'but God's first.'

The executioner asked for his forgiveness. More kissed him. 'Pick up thy spirits, man, and be not afraid to do thine office,' he said calmly. 'My neck is very short.'

He knelt, laid his head on the block and stretched out his arms. The executioner raised his axe, and Thomas More closed his eyes.

A moment later, the executioner's voice rang around the courtyard: 'Behold the head of a traitor!'

11

Madam, You Must Die

Horses clattered into the yard at Buckden Palace. Kneeling in prayer, Catherine of Aragon could hear heavy footsteps downstairs.

There was a knock at the door. The new Archbishop of York had arrived, and he was asking to see the former Queen.

Catherine knew why he had come, and by the time she swept in to see him she had assumed her most imperious manner. As the Archbishop began to explain the details of the new Act of Succession, she cut in.

There was no need to continue, she said icily. She had in her hand a copy of the Pope's judgement that her marriage had been perfectly legal. She was still Queen, and Mary was still the heir.

So the Archbishop should save his breath. She had no intention of swearing the oath.

When word of Catherine's refusal reached the court, Henry was not surprised. Knowing her as he did, he had never really expected her to swear it anyway.

Under the new law, Catherine was guilty of treason. So was Mary, who had also refused to swear. But even Henry recognized that executing his former wife and daughter would be political suicide, since it would almost certainly provoke an imperial invasion.

Catherine's defiance did not go unpunished, though. Any Spanish attendants who refused to swear the oath were ordered to leave England immediately.

Some had served her for more than a decade. One old retainer burst into tears as he knelt to say farewell, heartbroken 'to leave so good a mistress'.

A few days later, at the end of May 1534, Henry ordered Catherine to move house yet again. With her luggage packed onto carts, she was taken a few miles west, to the damp, decaying castle at Kimbolton.

Never had her fortunes been lower. She had lost her husband, her daughter, her title, her palaces, her gowns and most of her servants.

As in the long, gloomy years after the death of Arthur, she had no money and few possessions. And now her jewellery had been given to Anne Boleyn, leaving just her little statues of Catholic saints and an ornate Spanish crucifix.

At Kimbolton, she was barely more than a prisoner. She ate virtually nothing, and talked only to her chaplain and her doctor.

On fine afternoons she walked in the garden, head down, lost in thought. But she spent much of her time in her room, praying alone for hours on end, as pale and solemn as ever.

The years of disappointment had taken their toll. By the autumn of 1534, there were already rumours that Catherine was seriously ill.

Her daughter, Mary, whose own health had collapsed under the strain of her mistreatment, begged to visit her mother. But Henry always said no.

It would, of course, have cost him nothing, except perhaps a tongue-lashing from Anne. But he did not have it in him to be generous to the women he had betrayed.

The long, empty months passed, and fortune's wheel refused to turn. Catherine became weaker. News reached her that Thomas More was dead, and that Cromwell was beginning to close England's monasteries. All hope had vanished.

On 16 December 1535, Catherine marked her fiftieth birthday. The garden paradise of the Alhambra seemed very distant now.

As darkness fell on New Year's Day, a rider arrived outside the great house. Maria de Salinas was the last of the maidens who had sailed from Spain with Catherine, all those years ago. She had since married an English nobleman, but she and Catherine had remained the closest of friends.

For months Maria had been barred from seeing her old companion. But now, claiming that she had fallen off her horse and needed help, she pushed her way into the house. Everybody knew it was a trick, but there was not much they could do to stop her.

Maria was shocked by what she saw. Catherine was so ill she could barely sit up. Confined to her bed, she struggled to keep her food down and was in such pain that she lay awake all night, bathed in sweat, with barely a wink of sleep.

For the next few days, as Maria stayed by her side, Catherine sank fast. Too weak to write, she dictated a last letter to Henry. 'I forgive you,' she whispered, 'and pray God to do so likewise.'

On 6 January, Catherine briefly rallied. Before she went to sleep she was strong enough to brush and tie back her long fair hair, without help from Maria.

But in the dead of night she awoke, feeling worse than ever. She called for her doctor, and his stricken face told her everything she needed to know. 'Madam,' he said quietly, 'you must die.'

As dawn broke, Catherine took Mass one last time. She whispered a prayer for her servants, and asked God to 'pardon the King her husband for the wrong that he had done her'.

Her chaplain gave her the last rites. As Catherine lay in her friend Maria's arms, her breathing slowed.

The bare stone walls of Kimbolton began to fade. She could smell orange blossom in the Alhambra gardens. She could see her mother's face again; she could hear her sister's running footsteps.

It was Friday, 7 January 1536, and the girl from Castile had come home.

The news of Catherine's death reached Greenwich the very next day. Some people claimed to have seen Henry crying at her last letter, but others said he seemed overjoyed.

The Boleyns made no secret of their glee. Anne's father and brother joked that it was a pity Mary had not died, too.

The next day, Sunday, the royal couple put on a show of delight. As they led their courtiers into church, they both wore bright, tasteless yellow, and Henry had a jaunty feather in his cap.

After dinner, he visited Anne's apartments to dance with her ladies-in-waiting. Before he retired to bed, he sent for the two-year-old Elizabeth and proudly paraded her in his arms, as if to remind everybody whom he truly loved.

There was a strange, giddy atmosphere at the court that winter. To some observers, Henry seemed to be trying rather too hard to show how little he cared about his late wife.

But Anne seemed in excellent form. She was expecting another baby. Surely Henry would soon have the son he craved.

On 24 January, Henry went down to the tiltyard to practise his jousting. Clad in full armour, mounted on a huge charger, he thundered towards his opponent, the air trembling with the beat of his horse's hooves.

Closer and closer the two men came, their horses pounding faster and faster. Then came a shattering, splintering crack, as they collided in a blur of wood and metal and sweat and dust.

And then, suddenly, Henry was down, crashing on the ground, his huge horse rolling on top of him.

As he lay in a crumpled heap, some of his men feared the worst. The shock of the blow, the impact of the fall, the crushing weight of his horse – all this could kill a man in a moment.

Fortunately, he was still breathing. But he had fallen heavily, had suffered a nasty wound on the leg and had been knocked out cold. For two hours his companions tried to revive him, but without success.

And then, at last, he stirred. He could talk. He could move. He was all right.

In her chamber, Anne was sitting quietly with her ladies when the Duke of Norfolk arrived with the news. She listened in silence, but, as the colour drained from her face, everybody could see she was badly shaken.

The unhappy sequel came just five days later – the same day that Catherine of Aragon was laid to rest at Peterborough Cathedral.

At Greenwich, Anne had not recovered from the shock of Henry's fall. And when she felt an excruciatingly sharp pain below her stomach, she knew with chill certainty that fate had turned against her.

It was not the first time she had suffered a miscarriage, giving birth to a baby before it was ready for the world. But it was by far the most devastating.

She had been so confident, so certain she was carrying a boy. But once again, she had failed to give her husband the son he wanted.

When Henry heard the news, he did not bother to hide his disappointment. Almost in desperation, Anne sobbed that it must have been brought on by her shock at his jousting accident, which just proved how much she loved him.

Henry gazed at her, his eyes cold. 'I see that God will not give me male children,' he said.

Then, as if lashing out in panic, Anne snapped. It was all his fault, she shouted. She had seen him flirting with younger ladies at court. She had even seen him with a little maid of honour, Jane Seymour, sitting on his knee.

What was he thinking? Didn't he understand that if he treated his wife with such 'unkindness', disasters were bound to happen?

Her voice tailed off. Henry's face was hard.

She would need time to recover, he said coldly. After that, 'I will come and speak with you.'

Then he turned and walked away.

Anne and Henry had always had an extraordinarily fiery relationship. Right from the start, the King's love had burned with a white-hot flame, which is why he had been willing to risk so much for her.

But although plenty of men admired Anne's spirit, she

had a knack for making enemies. In an age when ladies were expected to say little and control their feelings, she had a quick temper and a sharp tongue.

Even with Henry, she could be very stormy company. Courtiers gossiped about her 'coldness and grumbling', and muttered that she ought to know her place.

But Henry was not exactly a model husband. When Anne told him off for flirting with other women, he snapped that 'she must shut her eyes and endure as those who were better than herself had done'. She ought to know, he added nastily, 'that he could at any time lower her as much as he had raised her'.

If Anne had given birth to a son, all the rows would have been forgotten, and her place would have been secure for ever. But the loss of her baby had been a shattering disappointment. And in Henry's manner, *something* – she could not quite say what – had changed.

Back in September, the couple had gone on a tour of south-western England. In Wiltshire they stayed with an old soldier, Sir John Seymour, at his country house, Wolf Hall.

It was there that Henry first noticed Seymour's daughter Jane, who had sometimes served as a lady-in-waiting at court. He thought little of it at the time. But after Anne's miscarriage, his mind turned more and more to the quiet young woman from Wolf Hall.

Anne and Jane could hardly have been more different. Anne was outspoken, spiky and suspicious. Jane was gentle, modest and good-natured. And for Henry, that was a refreshing change.

In the spring of 1536, while Jane was visiting Greenwich, he sent her a letter and a purse of sovereigns. But Jane returned the letter unopened, together with the purse.

She was, she explained, a 'gentlewoman of good and honourable parents'. She had 'nothing in the world but her honour, which for a thousand deaths she would not wound'.

So although she was flattered by Henry's attentions, she would never dream of becoming his mistress. If he really wanted to give her a present, perhaps he could wait until God had blessed her with a husband.

Far from being offended, Henry was charmed. At heart he remained an old-fashioned romantic, and he was delighted to find a young woman with such a noble character.

She had behaved 'very modestly', he said admiringly. In future, to show how much he respected her, he would only 'speak to her in the presence of some of her relatives'.

A little later, though, he wrote again, enclosing another gift and calling himself her 'devoted servant'. And this time, she kept the present.

By now, Anne was well aware what was going on. The court swirled with rumours of tantrums and rages behind the doors of her chamber.

Some people said the old nobles were using Jane as a weapon to get rid of Anne and bring Princess Mary back to court. In some versions, Henry himself had turned against Anne, convinced that she had bewitched him into marriage with her supernatural powers – which was why God had refused to give him a son.

To Anne, whose only crime had been to lose her baby,

stories like these were the stuff of nightmares. If they were true, everything she had worked for was slipping away. But there was very little she could do about them – not least because she had no privacy and no time to think.

At Henry's court, everything was public. Every day Anne had to perform. Every day there was another dance, another dinner, at which she had to wear her finest jewels and put on her most dazzling smile.

But all was not lost. After all, Henry had flirted with pretty favourites before, and nothing had happened. Anne still had friends and allies. She was still powerful. She was still Queen.

It was then that she made her fatal mistake.

Sunday, 2 April was Passion Sunday, an important date in the build-up to Easter. At Greenwich, the court filed into the Chapel Royal for the usual service.

The preacher for the day was Anne's chaplain, John Skip. And as his listeners settled back in their pews, Skip began by reminding them of the tale of Esther, a Jewish maiden who marries the Persian king Ahasuerus.

In the original Bible story, Ahasuerus is misled by his sinister adviser Haman, who bribes him to kill all the Jews.

But in Skip's version, Haman persuades him to kill the Jews in order to steal the money from them afterwards.

The two versions end the same way. Esther intervenes to save her people. Ahasuerus realizes the error of his ways, and Haman is hanged high from a gallows.

As Skip's voice rang across the chapel, everybody knew who he was really talking about. Ahasuerus was Henry. Esther was Anne. And the wicked Haman was the King's Chief Secretary, Thomas Cromwell.

To Cromwell, Skip's sermon was more than open defiance. It was Anne's declaration of war.

On paper, Anne and Cromwell should have been allies. Both supported the break with Rome; both had embraced the new Protestant ideas.

But in recent weeks, they had fallen out about the future of England's monasteries. As Vicar-General, Cromwell had drawn up a plan to shut most of the monasteries down, seizing their lands and money for the King. That would solve Henry's money problems for ever, making him rich beyond his wildest dreams.

But Anne had her own plans for the money, which she wanted to spend on schools and help for the poor. In her mind, she was England's Protestant champion, and this mere brewer's son should know his place.

But if she thought Thomas Cromwell was going to surrender, she had misjudged her man.

He had his own reasons for loathing Anne. He had never forgiven her for the downfall of his old master Cardinal Wolsey, all those years ago.

But Cromwell was also a brilliant chess player. Few men were better at judging which moves would bring victory closer, and which would be too risky; which pieces to keep, and which to sacrifice.

With her outbursts and temper tantrums, Anne was a dangerous figurehead for the Protestant cause. She was too unreliable, too unpopular. Even Martin Luther thought Henry had been wrong to discard Catherine for her.

If Henry was losing interest in her, that made her a problem. And now she was going to cause trouble for Cromwell about the monasteries, too.

So, as Cromwell studied the chessboard, there seemed an obvious solution. Since Henry had a fancy for this Seymour girl, wouldn't it be easiest just to ditch Anne completely?

Moving against Anne would be enormously risky, though. If it went wrong, Cromwell would end up on the chopping block.

For two weeks he brooded. Then a small but pivotal moment made his mind up for him.

For almost thirty years, England had trodden a fine line between the Continent's two superpowers, France and the Holy Roman Empire. Personally, Cromwell had always favoured an alliance with the Empire, but the tortured business of Henry's divorce from the Emperor's aunt had made that impossible.

With Catherine dead, there was a chance for a fresh start. If Henry would agree to bring Mary back to court and join the Emperor's war against the French, the Emperor might offer a new alliance.

On 18 April, Cromwell arranged a meeting between Henry and the imperial ambassador. To his horror, though, Henry behaved atrociously.

No, he said angrily, he would not bring Mary back. No, he would not help the Emperor against the French.

In fact, he would not make any compromise at all, unless the Emperor recognized Anne as Queen and supported Henry's claim to be Supreme Head of the Church. And since the Emperor was never going to do that, there would be no alliance.

Cromwell left the meeting trembling with rage. He had spent months arranging a deal. And now Henry had ruined it, all because of his blasted marriage to that wretched Boleyn.

That night Cromwell sat up late, deep in thought. The next day, he met the imperial ambassador again to discuss the way forward. For a while both men seemed sunk in gloom.

Then, suddenly, Cromwell smiled.

'The game,' he said softly, 'is not entirely lost.'

He had made up his mind. Anne had to go. And he had just worked out how to do it.

12

Death, Rock Me Asleep

On a sunny Saturday in April, Anne walked into her outer chamber at Greenwich to find a handsome young man standing near the window, apparently lost in a daydream.

Mark Smeaton had been born in the Low Countries. A fine singer and a 'deft dancer', he had moved to England in his teens to become a musician.

He was popular at court, and Anne had once asked him to play for her. But as a mere servant, Mark was never part of her inner circle.

Now something in his manner caught Anne's attention, and she asked why he seemed so sad.

Smeaton sighed. It was 'no matter', he said, in the mournful tone of a lovesick teenager talking to his idol.

Anne bristled. He was just a musician, with no right to talk to her in this way.

'You may not look to have me speak to you as I should do to a nobleman,' she snapped, 'because you are an inferior person.'

'No, no, madam,' Smeaton said hastily, 'a look sufficed

me.' And with Anne's eyes boring into his back, he strolled away.

It was nothing really: the kind of silly little incident that happened all the time at court.

Anne and her friends were always pretending to fall in love with each other, as if acting out the stories of Lancelot and Guinevere. This was the game of courtly love, played in palaces all over Europe.

As a mere musician, Smeaton was not supposed to join in. It was not a crime, though; just a cheeky joke. By the evening, Anne would probably have forgotten all about it.

But when his spy reported the conversation a few hours later, Thomas Cromwell gave a grim nod.

This was just what he needed. Now for the next step.

The next day, Sunday 30 April, found the court preparing for the May Day celebrations. Despite his accident, Henry had planned another lavish tournament, and in the tiltyard his servants were making the final arrangements.

Anne spent the day at the palace. At one point she caught sight of Sir Henry Norris, one of the King's closest companions.

Norris was a jolly, well-liked fellow. He was supposed

·to be marrying Anne's cousin, but he had never got around to doing it. Anne asked him what was going on.

Norris shrugged. He was in no hurry. He preferred to wait.

Anne smirked. 'You look for dead men's shoes,' she said coyly. If anything happened to Henry, 'you would look to have me'.

Of course, she was not serious. She thought she was being witty and flirtatious.

But Norris went pale. Under Cromwell's new laws, it was treason even to joke about the King's death. If he had 'any such thought', he said hastily, he would rather 'his head were off'.

Anne's face darkened. She hated to be contradicted, and snapped that she could easily 'undo him' if she wanted.

Norris snapped back at her; their tempers rose; and suddenly they were having a full-blown argument.

Henry found out about it later that afternoon. He was not pleased, and later he and Anne had a ferocious row.

This was nothing unusual. Their relationship had always been stormy, but they usually patched it up afterwards.

But in the meantime, Cromwell was busy. That afternoon, he had summoned Mark Smeaton to his house in Stepney, a village just to the east of London.

No sooner had Smeaton stepped through the door than he felt muscular arms grabbing him from behind. He tried to struggle, but Cromwell's men were too strong for him.

In front of him, the Secretary stood calmly, a half-smile on his lips. He gestured to his men.

One of them tied a knotted rope around the young musician's head. Then he began to tighten it, until the pain was so great that Smeaton was screaming for mercy.

'Ah, Mark,' Cromwell said gently. 'If you do not tell me all the truth, I swear by the life of the King I will torture you till you do.'

Again the man tightened the rope, and Smeaton's screams rang around the room.

'Sir Secretary, no more, I will tell the truth!' he shrieked. 'No more, sir, I will tell you everything that has happened!'

Cromwell smiled, and leaned forward.

The next day was May Day. At Greenwich, Henry's friends were looking forward to the jousting.

Henry himself was the picture of good-humoured generosity. When his friend Norris's horse refused to charge, he offered him one of his own instead.

Anne, too, seemed to have forgotten their argument. As the contestants thundered past on their mighty mounts, she waved from the Queen's box, hung with cloth of gold.

The jousting was well underway when Anne noticed a flurry of activity at her husband's side. An attendant handed him a note. Henry opened it and began to read, his face expressionless.

Anne turned her attention back to the jousting. The last knight galloped down the lists, and the tournament was over. She glanced across at her husband. Henry was on his feet, his servants around him. He did not look at her.

Beside the tiltyard, where the contestants were pulling off their armour, Henry Norris was chatting to a friend when he saw the guards. 'Sir, the King calls you,' their captain said.

Norris frowned. There was some mistake, surely?

Back in the Queen's box, Anne and her ladies were ready to leave. In the distance, she could hear the clatter of hooves. Henry and his men were riding towards London. Somewhere Norris was among them, his face white and shaken.

For a moment, Anne felt a chill of anxiety. Why was Henry in such a hurry to go back to London? Why had he not said goodbye?

Then she shrugged, and led her ladies towards her apartments. Perhaps he was still cross about yesterday's argument. She would find out soon enough.

That night, Anne slept in her bedchamber at Greenwich. It was the last night she would ever spend as a free woman.

The next morning, Anne was watching a game of tennis when a messenger appeared at her shoulder. The King's councillors had arrived at the palace and would like to see her.

When Anne left the tennis court, she found her uncle, the Duke of Norfolk, waiting with the other councillors. In his early sixties, Norfolk saw himself as the leader of the old noble families. He was a hard, ruthless man: a born survivor, a shameless plotter who would do whatever it took to cling onto his place on the ladder.

He had always been fond of Anne, but now he wasted no time. She was under arrest for high treason, having conspired with Mark Smeaton and Henry Norris to murder her husband.

For a moment, as the room spun around her, Anne could not believe it. It must be a sick joke, or some sort of ghastly mistake.

Norfolk was still talking. Smeaton had already confessed, so there was no point in denying it. She would be taken to the Tower of London. They would leave as soon as the river tide turned.

Anne was talking, babbling, protesting her innocence. She felt dizzy. She felt sick. But Norfolk brushed her words aside. 'Tut, tut,' he said impatiently, as if talking to a naughty child.

Everything was happening so quickly. Anne's mind was reeling, and she was struggling to think.

A plot to kill her husband? It was mad, unthinkable! If only she could speak to Henry, she could explain everything.

Norfolk shook his head. No.

They left early that afternoon, the barge ploughing through the murky waters. Ahead glowered the stone fastness of the Tower, its high walls blank and forbidding.

The riverbanks were empty, the air heavy with dread. The light was fading. It was not cold, but Anne was shivering.

At the Tower, the Constable, Sir William Kingston, awaited his royal guest. When Anne climbed up the steps, he could see she was close to collapse.

'Mr Kingston,' she said, her voice trembling, 'shall I go into a dungeon?'

'No, madam,' Kingston said gently. 'You shall go into the lodging you lay in at your coronation.'

'It is too good for me,' Anne said, and then her voice broke. 'Jesu have mercy upon me!' She fell to her knees, her body racked by terrible sobs. Then she started laughing manically, as if she was losing her mind.

She looked up at the Constable. 'Mr Kingston,' she said desperately, 'shall I die without justice?'

Kingston frowned. 'The poorest subject the King has,' he said, 'has justice.'

At that, he later remembered, Anne started laughing again.

In the next few days, Cromwell's agents rounded up the other supposed plotters. They had Smeaton, they had Norris and now they had Anne's brother George, too.

In the Tower, Anne could not stop talking. Swinging between violent weeping fits and shrill, hysterical laughter, she babbled out a shower of names, as if desperate to find the words that would save her from death.

Kingston duly noted down the names and passed them to the authorities.

Sir Francis Weston, now! He had always been such a character: a joker, a playboy, a bit of a rogue. Anne remembered him telling her that he loved her more than his own wife.

Weston was arrested two days later.

Then there was William Brereton. He had never been a close friend of Anne's, so it was hard to believe that he had been part of any plot. But he and Cromwell had never got along.

Brereton was arrested at the same time as Weston.

Who else? A real conspiracy would have more than six people. So a week later, Cromwell's agents arrested Anne's friend Sir Richard Page, as well as her old admirer, the poet Thomas Wyatt.

But Cromwell never seriously intended to put those two on trial. It was good to have a couple of extra suspects, but they were decent fellows and he always planned to let them go.

All the time, Anne wept. She had always been a woman of strong feelings, and now she felt fear surging through her, drowning her, suffocating her.

She could not understand what had happened. It was as if the ground beneath her feet had crumbled into nothingness. How could Henry believe she had been plotting with a nobody like Mark Smeaton?

Perhaps her husband was testing her, and would welcome her back once she had shown her loyalty. 'I think the King does it to prove me,' she told the Constable, with feverish brightness.

And then she started laughing again, and was 'very merry'.

But Henry was not testing her. Just as he had convinced himself that he had never really been married to Catherine, so he was certain now that Anne was false.

When he thought about Cromwell's note, which was the first he had heard of the conspiracy, tears of self-pity welled up in his eyes.

The witch had been lying to him from the start! He had never really loved her, but she had used her wiles to lure him away from 'good Queen Catherine'. That was why God had not given them a son.

It all added up. No doubt she had used her evil skills to murder Catherine, and she must have been planning to poison poor Mary, too.

He had been shocked, of course, when Cromwell told him about Smeaton's confession. He had been shocked about Harry Norris, too.

But when they left the tournament that day, he could tell from Norris's desperate gabbling that he was guilty. That was a reminder that a king could never trust anybody, not even his friends.

But now, thank goodness, Henry could move on. He would let justice take its course, and forget all about the witch Anne.

Indeed, he had already found the ideal person to take her place. Polite, kind, gentle, honourable – could there be a better wife than Jane Seymour?

The trial of Smeaton, Norris, Weston and Brereton opened at Westminster Hall on Friday, 12 May.

It was a total sham. Smeaton had confessed, but only after agonizing torture. The other three maintained their innocence – even Norris, who had been promised a royal pardon if he confessed.

But the judges, a panel of the most eminent noblemen in the land, had made up their minds beforehand. Cromwell had provided the evidence. Henry wanted them dead. So there was nothing to discuss.

The verdicts came down: Guilty. Guilty. Guilty. Guilty. Then the sentence: Death. Death. Death. Death.

Three days later, Anne's guards led her into the Tower of London's Great Hall, where her trial was due to begin. Thousands of spectators were packed into the special grandstands, keen to see the show.

As they saw the flash of the Queen's gown in the doorway, the excited chatter died away. Anne glanced anxiously around her. The Great Hall was a sea of faces: curious, puzzled, hostile, excited . . . but none of them friendly.

On the platform sat the judges, more than two dozen lords of England. Her uncle, the Duke of Norfolk, was in charge, his face dark and set. But there was no Henry, and no Cromwell.

Norfolk rose to his feet, his voice echoing around the hall. Anne was accused of the most terrible crimes.

She had conspired with her brother and four other men to murder the King and marry Norris. She had given the plotters bribes to secure their loyalty. She had poisoned Catherine, and she had been planning to poison Mary.

Anne shook her head. This was madness.

After her tears in the Tower, she now seemed oddly calm, her answers low and clear. Like Catherine, her old enemy, she had saved her finest performance for the greatest stage.

She denied everything. The only shred of truth in the judges' story was that she had given presents to Francis

Weston. But she had given presents to lots of people. It hardly meant she was plotting to murder her husband.

It was useless, though. Norfolk called for the judges' verdicts, starting with the youngest, Harry Percy.

Percy and Anne had been very close when they were young, and he had been keen to marry her. Many people thought he was still in love with her.

Now Percy's face was a mask of anguish. He knew what the King expected of him. There was a long pause. Norfolk repeated the question.

'Guilty,' Percy said, his voice dull and hopeless.

Guilty. Guilty. Guilty. Guilty . . .

Norfolk went last. 'Guilty.'

He looked at his niece, and she was surprised to see tears in his eyes. He began reading from a piece of parchment:

'Because thou hast offended against our sovereign the King's Grace in committing treason against his person, and here attainted of the same, the law of the realm is this, that thou hast deserved death . . .'

But by then Anne had stopped listening.

The first four defendants, as well as Anne's brother George, were beheaded at Tower Hill on the following Wednesday.

Anne was due to die the next day. Henry had agreed that as a special favour, she would not be burned, but beheaded with a sword, as befitted a queen.

He had arranged to bring over a special executioner from Calais, who was supposed to be the best in the business. His fee was £24, a lot of money in those days, but he was meant to be worth it.

At the Tower, Anne seemed in good spirits. As Kingston reported, his prisoners were usually in 'great sorrow', but she sometimes seemed to find 'joy and pleasure in death'.

In truth, she was ready for the end. Her game was over, and she had lost. One evening she scribbled a little poem:

> *O death, rock me asleep,*
> *Bring me the quiet rest;*
> *Let pass my weary guiltless ghost*
> *Out of my careful breast:*
> *Toll on the passing bell,*
> *Ring out the doleful knell,*
> *Let thy sound my death tell,*
> *Death doth draw nigh;*
> *There is no remedy.*

At dawn on Thursday, Archbishop Cranmer arrived to pray with the Queen for the final time. But by mid-morning the guards had still not come, and Anne complained to Kingston that she had expected to be 'dead and past my pain' by now.

He admitted that the execution had been postponed till the next day, which he knew was cruel. But it would be very quick, he said hastily. 'It should be no pain, it was so subtle.'

Anne smiled. 'I heard say the executioner was very good,' she said, 'and I have a little neck.' She put her hands around her throat, and laughed.

The following morning, Friday, 19 May, Anne was led onto Tower Green. The authorities had chosen a quiet spot, in order to keep crowds away.

But Henry's councillors were there, their faces grave. A few feet away stood Thomas Cromwell. His features betrayed no satisfaction; just the usual unreadable calm.

As the captain led Anne up to the scaffold, she seemed tired and dazed. She wore a fur mantle over a loose fur-trimmed grey gown, and a plain white cap beneath her boxy headdress.

She turned to the spectators. 'Good Christian people,' she said clearly. 'I am come hither to die . . .

'I pray God save the King, and send him long to reign over you, for there never was a gentler, nor a more merciful prince. And to me he was ever a good, a gentle, and sovereign lord.'

She knelt upright. Her ladies removed her mantle. She

took off her hood and tucked her hair into her coif, a white linen cap, and arranged her gown about her feet.

She seemed very frightened now. The executioner whispered: 'Madam, do not fear, I will wait till you tell me.'

One of the ladies tied a blindfold over her eyes. 'To Jesus Christ I commend my soul,' Anne said, her voice shaking.

The spectators fell to their knees. The executioner reached for the sword, which had been hidden in the straw on the platform.

Anne was murmuring prayers over and over again: 'O Lord God, have pity on my soul. Jesus, receive my soul . . .'

The executioner's assistant called out: 'Bring me the sword!', and Anne instinctively turned her head towards him.

At that moment, the executioner stepped noiselessly behind her. He raised the sword high above his head, half-turned his shoulders, and swung it down with devastating speed.

A moment later, the cannons boomed on the walls of the Tower. It was done.

In the next few days, people reported strange signs and omens across the land.

At Peterborough Cathedral, where Catherine of Aragon had been buried, the candles surrounding her tomb had unexpectedly burst into flame that morning. At the very moment the sword fell, they suddenly went out.

That evening, people saw hares running in the fields. They all knew the hare was the sign of the witch. And every year, on the anniversary of Anne's death, they heard hares screaming in the night.

At the Tower, Thomas Wyatt had watched Anne's final moments from his cell window. Afterwards, mourning the woman he had loved, he wrote one of his most famous poems:

These bloody days have broken my heart.
My lust, my youth did them depart . . .

Eleven days later, Henry married again.

PART THREE

JANE SEYMOUR

13

Jane the Fair

The morning after Anne Boleyn's execution, a barge pushed away from the north bank of the Thames, heading upriver towards the great palace of Hampton Court.

Aboard, a pale, fair-haired young woman wrapped her cloak about her shoulders and gazed out at the shimmering waters.

As a girl growing up in the Wiltshire countryside, Jane Seymour had never dreamed of marrying a king. Her father, old Sir John, was known as a quiet, sensible fellow, living peacefully with his family at his country house, Wolf Hall.

As for Jane, nobody had a bad word to say about her. The imperial ambassador reported that she was 'of middle height and no great beauty', but like everybody else, he was impressed by her gentle character.

She was kind. She was nice. She was ordinary. And that, it turned out, was just what the King wanted.

When the barge reached Hampton Court, servants were waiting to bring her upstairs. Henry was in no mood to hang around. By the afternoon, he and Jane had been formally betrothed.

As the couple joined hands to seal their promise, it was hard to believe that just three weeks earlier, Henry and Anne had been watching the jousting together. Everything had happened so fast, the wheel of fortune turning with dizzying speed.

On 30 May, Henry and Jane were secretly married in the Queen's Chamber at Whitehall. As at his second wedding, there were no guests.

The following Friday, they moved on to Greenwich, where Anne had been watching tennis before her arrest a month earlier. And two days later, Jane led the courtiers to Sunday service, just as her predecessor had done a few weeks before.

Even at the time, people wondered what was going through Jane's mind. Did she spare a thought for the dark-eyed woman who, until recently, had lived in the same rooms and slept in the same bed?

When she closed her eyes at night, did she think of the prisoner kneeling in terror before the executioner on Tower Green? Did she never fear that one day, she too might suffer the same terrible fate?

But Jane gave nothing away. She remained as calm, polite and even-tempered as ever, showing no flicker of fear or doubt.

At first, some people thought it must be an act, and that secretly she must be just as calculating as everybody else. But soon they realized that she was not acting at all. In a world of silken schemers, Jane was the only person with nothing to hide.

On 7 June, she made her first major outing as Queen, joining Henry on his barge as he returned to Westminster. The banks of the Thames were packed with sightseers, the waters crowded with boats and barges.

Halfway to the City, they passed the imperial ambassador's house. In a show of support, he stepped down to the bank to salute them, while his personal trumpeters greeted them with a deafening fanfare.

As the trumpets' blare faded into the distance, Jane recognized the bleak fastness of the Tower of London. But now, as the sun sparkled on the choppy waters, its walls were draped with banners and streamers.

As the royal barge came into view, the cannons boomed in mighty celebration – just as they had a few weeks earlier, on a much darker royal occasion.

The crowds cheered. Jane grinned and waved. And in an unmarked grave behind the vast stone walls, Anne Boleyn's body lay silent and cold.

For Catherine of Aragon's daughter, Mary, locked up in a Hertfordshire manor house and still mourning her mother's death, Anne's downfall had been wonderful news. And there was better to come.

To Jane, it seemed dreadful that the King's eldest daughter should be banished from court. As soon as she was married, she fell to her knees and begged Henry to bring Mary back into the fold, so that they could be one happy family.

At first, Henry said no. But he had always had a sentimental side, and he rather enjoyed hearing his kind-hearted wife pleading for her stepdaughter. If nothing else, it reminded him how different she was from Anne.

But there was a condition – the same old condition, in fact. Mary had to sign a document admitting that her parents had never been truly married, and recognizing her father as Supreme Head of the Church.

As stubborn as ever, Mary said no. But her conviction was wavering. Her mother was dead, and Anne was dead, and Jane was desperate for her to come back.

Eventually, after weeks of argument, Mary agreed to sign. She still did not believe a word of it; but now, thank goodness, the breach was over.

For Jane, and perhaps even for Henry, this was a moment of sweet relief. And Mary soon had her reward. In the next few days, presents poured into the Hertfordshire manor house: clothes, books, even a horse.

Early on 6 July, while it was still dark, horsemen arrived at her house and ordered her to come with them. Their destination was the village of Hackney, north of London.

A few hours later, a huge, heavy figure appeared in the doorway of the chamber where Mary waited. It was the King.

For the first time in five years, father and daughter embraced. Both were in tears. Henry was so carried away he could not stop talking, promising her anything she wanted.

Behind him, wreathed in smiles, stood Jane, who had made it possible. She held out her hands to Mary, then produced a present: a sparkling diamond ring, to show how much she loved her new daughter.

Henry had brought a present, too: a pouch of a thousand crowns 'for her little pleasures'. For the rest of the evening, and much of the next day, the three of them talked. And it was settled. Catherine's daughter was coming home.

A few days later, the Lady Mary took her place at court. All eyes were on her: a thin, short, reddish-haired young woman of twenty, with her mother's deep voice and solemn features.

At dinner she sat in a place of honour, opposite her new stepmother. There were only seven years between them, so they might easily have become rivals.

But Jane knew how badly Mary had suffered. She recognized how lonely she was, and how sad. She saw that if only Mary had somebody she could trust, she might relax and open up.

In the next few weeks, Jane went out of her way to treat her stepdaughter kindly, and they soon became fast friends. They sent each other presents, not just expensive treats like jewels and clothes, but little things, like fresh cucumbers for their tea.

So life at court found a new balance, a new harmony. Even Jane's personal motto, 'Bound to obey and serve', captured the mood.* Nobody could imagine Anne choosing anything like that.

Jane was 'as gentle a lady as I ever knew', wrote one courtier, 'and as fair a Queen as any in Christendom'. And in her own quiet way, she seemed as happy as could be.

Every week Henry presented her with diamonds and pearls, emeralds and rubies. He even gave her a magnificent golden cup, designed by the great painter Hans Holbein, and inscribed with her personal motto and their initials, entwined in a lover's knot.

At heart, though, Jane was a woman of simple pleasures. She adored horses and owned a white poodle. She liked to sit quietly with her needlework and embroidery. And she loved gardening, especially in the magnificent grounds of Hampton Court.

---

* Queens were expected to choose their own personal motto. Perhaps everybody should have one these days.

As for Henry, he seemed liberated after the months of squabbling. Once again he threw himself into the pursuit of pleasure, from dances and parties to hunting and tennis.

Yet his courtiers could not help noticing that at forty-five, he was not as young as he had been. The wound on his leg, dating back to his tournament accident, had never properly healed. Sometimes he walked with a limp, and eagle-eyed observers spotted him wincing in pain.

Above all, though, Henry was putting on weight. A few months after his wedding, he commissioned Holbein to paint a magnificent portrait of him, to go on the wall at York Place.

Holbein painted the King in a sumptuous, broad-shouldered velvet robe, his muscular legs braced wide apart. His narrow eyes gaze coldly ahead. He looks every inch a king and emperor.

But he is also very fat. His cheeks are enormous; his beard barely hides his collection of chins; even his fingers are thick and stubby.

In Henry's heart, too, something had changed. The fun-loving young man who had married Catherine was long gone now.

Over the years he had become distrustful, impatient and arrogant. 'He never forgets his own greatness,' wrote a French visitor, 'and is silent as to that of others.'

In Henry's mind, he stood supreme, the master of all. No man should defy him; no woman should disagree with him. If they did, the penalty was death.

But thousands of his subjects thought differently. And just a few weeks after the Lady Mary's return, the long years of tension reached boiling point.

The summer of 1536 had been kind to Thomas Cromwell. As he sat back at his desk, piled high with letters and documents, he could reflect on a game well played and a job well done.

With his usual ruthless cunning, he had checkmated Anne Boleyn, avenged the death of Wolsey and made himself more useful to the King than ever. Despite his Protestant beliefs, he had even worked hard to get on well with Mary.

Amid all the excitement, Cromwell had never lost sight of his goal. He remained committed to his dream of a truly Protestant England, in which men and women would read the Bible for themselves, and the privileges of the Pope and his priests would be swept away for ever.

Much had been done already. England had broken with Rome. Henry was head of the Church. Every week, new books arrived from Germany and the Low Countries, while preachers poured scorn on pilgrimage, the saints, Purgatory and the Mass.

But much remained to be done. Cromwell knew books and sermons were not enough. To flourish, the new Protestant England would need a strong, well-organized government, with agents all over the country.

He had great plans. He dreamed of new laws and new schools, new roads and new bridges, schemes to improve trade, farming and help for the poor.

But to do all this, the King needed cash. And Cromwell knew where to get it.

England's monasteries, abbeys and nunneries were some of the biggest landowners in the country. There were almost a thousand in total, although some of them were very small, housing about 10,000 monks and 2,000 nuns.

People had been complaining about the monasteries for years. They were supposed to be houses of prayer, yet they had built up immense wealth.

Traditionally, monks were meant to spend their days praying, caring for the sick and devoting themselves to God. But to their critics, many of them were fat, greedy and lazy. And since they were loyal to the Pope, many Protestants saw them as an enemy within.

For Cromwell, all this made them the perfect target.

With one blow, he would make Henry rich, strengthen his own position and smash one of the last bastions of Catholic power in England.

In the autumn of 1535, he sent forth his agents to hammer on the monasteries' doors. They had orders to note down anything even slightly suspicious: forged accounts, fake relics, dodgy miracles and, in particular, greedy behaviour by the monks themselves.

Within weeks their reports were piling up on Cromwell's desk. And to his grim satisfaction, two things leaped out.

To begin with, all monks had sworn an oath not to marry. They were meant to have no time for women, just as nuns, the 'brides of Christ', were supposed to have nothing to do with men.

But Cromwell's agents found countless cases of monks chasing local women, nuns and even other monks. They even found numerous nuns who had secretly had children, which was not exactly an ideal advertisement for marriage to Jesus.

The other remarkable finding was that so many of the monasteries' treasured relics were ludicrous fakes. Even Cromwell's agents could not help smirking at some of the so-called relics.

At Maiden Bradley Priory in Wiltshire, they confiscated the Virgin Mary's dress, 'God's coat' and 'part of God's supper', as well as the stone on which Jesus had been born. And at Bury St Edmunds they found 'enough pieces of the holy cross to make a whole cross', as well as St Edmund's toenails, St Thomas's penknife and the coals on which St Lawrence had been burned alive.

For Cromwell, this was too good to be true. The monasteries were not merely corrupt, they were ridiculous. And as always, he moved with ruthless decisiveness.

In the spring of 1536, he persuaded Parliament to pass a law shutting down all the smaller establishments and handing their wealth and property to the King. It was an attack not just on hundreds of monasteries, but on the life of Catholic England. But because Cromwell had Henry's backing, there was nothing the monks could do about it.

News of the decision rippled like a shockwave across the English countryside. For people far from London, this was much more horrifying than the news about Anne Boleyn or Jane Seymour.

The monks were far from perfect, and many of the abbeys were pretty sleepy places. But to countless ordinary people, these buildings were a central part of their little local world.

For generations people had gone to their local abbeys to buy bread, honey or beer, or to do odd jobs for the monks, or just to pray or ask for advice. Many had friends or relatives who were monks or nuns. They enjoyed seeing their splendid buildings, their lovingly assembled libraries, their magnificent windows and soaring ceilings.

But now, almost overnight, hundreds of monasteries were being shut down. There were even rumours that soon Cromwell would come for the ordinary parish churches, which stood at the heart of English village life.

For many people, all this was too much to bear. And that autumn, they cracked.

William Breyar was on the run.

Breyar was a hardened criminal. His hand had been seared with a red-hot brand, leaving a mark to warn people of his record. Now he was moving north, staying away from the main thoroughfares, keeping to the narrow, shaded lanes where he might not be spotted.

By September 1536, Breyar had reached the green valleys of the Yorkshire Dales. During his journey he had stolen a large badge that identified him as a King's man: the ideal way, he thought, to impress the locals.

One morning, Breyar trudged into the village of Dent. The place seemed unusually busy, buzzing with chatter and excitement, but he thought little of it.

Then he felt a blow on his shoulder. He turned, and saw the local blacksmith, smeared with soot. The blacksmith was pointing at his badge, his face red and angry.

Here, shouted the blacksmith, was a King's man! He pushed his face into Breyar's. 'Thy master is a thief,' he yelled, 'for he pulleth down all our churches in the country.'

Breyar opened his mouth to defend himself, but by now

a crowd had gathered, and some of them began shouting and arguing. It wasn't Breyar's fault, they said. 'It is not the King's deed but the deed of Crumwell. If we had him here we would crum him and crum him that he was never so crummed.'

Dumbly, Breyar nodded. And as the villagers continued to argue among themselves, he picked his moment to slip away.

A few hours later he staggered into the town of Kirkby Lonsdale and demanded to see the local magistrate. He had valuable information, he said, about a rebellion deep in the Dales.

But the magistrate already knew all about it. For weeks the people of Dent, like their neighbours in the surrounding villages, had been convinced that 'Crumwell' was about to destroy their churches. They had sworn an oath that when his agents arrived, they would stand and fight.

Dent was a tiny place, of course. But it was not alone. Hundreds of miles away, on the eastern edge of England, another fire was being lit.

No village in England was prouder of its local church than Louth, in the gently rolling hills of the Lincolnshire Wolds. Twenty years earlier, its people had raised a colossal £305 – the equivalent of at least two million pounds today – to put up the tallest spire in the country.

But with Cromwell's agents due in town, Louth's beloved church seemed to be under threat. And when, on Sunday 1 October, the vicar stepped into the pulpit, he had chilling news.

This might be the villagers' last chance, he warned, to see their beloved church's treasures. For when Cromwell's men arrived, the treasures would be gone.

By the time the service ended, passions were boiling over. Outside, villagers paraded with the church's great silver crosses, shouting that they would never let them be taken. One man, pretending to draw a dagger, yelled that he would 'make the King and his masters a breakfast such as they had never had'.

That evening, some of them gathered outside, carrying makeshift weapons. As their leader they chose the shoe-maker, who called himself Captain Cobbler, and posted sentries in the church overnight.

By the following morning, Louth was in uproar. In the streets, armed villagers were searching for strangers. Outside the church, Captain Cobbler and his friends were feeding a bonfire with copies of the 'new books'. And all the time, the church bells rang, summoning nearby villages to join the rebellion.

At first, as the bells rang out across the fields of Lincolnshire, there came no answer. There was nothing, just the trill of birdsong and the crackle of the bonfire.

And then, in the distance, came a faint but unmistakable sound. *Ding-dong, ding-dong, ding-dong* . . .

Louth's call had been heard. At long last, England was rising.

14

The Grand Captain

Three days after Louth rose up, a man called Robert Aske set out from his sister's house in Yorkshire for the long ride south.

It had been a jolly party, and his sister's family had been in excellent form. But all good things must come to an end, and Aske was needed in London, where he worked as a lawyer.

You could hardly have found a more ordinary man than Robert Aske. In his thirty-six years, he had made no great impression on the world.

Although he came from a comfortable Yorkshire family, he was neither rich nor powerful. The only thing people noticed about him was that he was blind in one eye.

Like countless other people across the North, Aske had watched the dramatic changes of recent years with confusion and alarm.

He had always been a loyal Catholic, and had felt sorry for Catherine of Aragon and her daughter, Mary. He could not understand why Henry had broken with Rome, and was appalled by Cromwell's attack on the monasteries.

And he had heard all the strange rumours about Henry's

true nature. When Aske was a boy, he had heard the prophecy of the Mouldwarp – a wicked, accursed creature, a giant mole with the skin of a goat, who would one day become king and lead England to disaster.

According to legend, it was the wizard Merlin who had first foreseen the coming of the Mouldwarp. Now people whispered that Henry was the Mouldwarp, and that it would all end in terrible slaughter.

Aske was not so sure. Deep down, he blamed Cromwell and his wicked councillors, not the King. Get rid of them, and Henry would lead his people back to the true path.

But this was all pointless. Aske was just an ordinary lawyer. There was nothing he could do about it.

Now he spurred his horse. The dark waters of the Humber were coming into view, and beyond them the fields of Lincolnshire. He had a long way to go before he reached London.

The rebels captured Aske that evening, as he rode south past Sawcliff Farm. He had heard rumours of the uprising from the Humber ferryman, and had been hoping to skirt the worst of the trouble and get back to his sister's house, abandoning his journey south.

But now, surrounded by more than a dozen men on horseback, Aske knew it was useless to resist. Indeed, when he listened to their hoarse explanations, he found himself half-agreeing with them.

The next day, the men rode inland, taking Aske with them. They treated him with wary respect, and he no longer felt afraid. So when they halted at Kirton that afternoon, unsure what to do next, he impulsively offered to ride towards Louth and speak to the rebels there.

Even as he spoke, Aske could hear a voice in his head, asking what on earth he was playing at. He was a lawyer, sworn to obey the King. What was he doing, carrying messages for a gang of rebels he barely knew?

But another inner voice, louder and stronger, urged him to do it. Didn't he agree with everything these men said? What harm could it do?

Everything went according to plan. Aske made contact with the other group, and returned to the men at Kirton. Pleased and relieved, they told him he was free to go, and he turned his horse towards Yorkshire.

And that was that. His part in the little drama was over, and he could ride back to his sister's house and forget all about it.

For Robert Aske, though, it was far from over.

In London, word of the uprising had reached the court on the morning of 4 October, the same day that Aske first set out.

Faced with the most dangerous rebellion he had ever known, Henry was aghast. He immediately wrote to the Duke of Norfolk, the most powerful nobleman in England, urging him to gather his men and head north as soon as possible.

Meanwhile the court was in uproar. Soldiers were rushing everywhere, collecting horses and gathering weapons.

But as Henry's soldiers marched north, the rebellion was spiralling out of control. With church bells tolling across Lincolnshire, the rebels published a list of demands, including the restoration of the abbeys and the execution of Cromwell.

Already the uprising had claimed its first victims: a church officer beaten to death in Horncastle, a suspected royal spy hanged from a tree. And on 6 October the rebels marched into the city of Lincoln, smashing and looting the Bishop's Palace.

Five days later the first royal army, commanded by the Duke of Suffolk, crossed the border into Lincolnshire. But at this point, faced with the reality of battle, the rebels lost their nerve. When Suffolk ordered them to disperse, most of them meekly agreed.

Henry was in no mood to be forgiving. In secret, he instructed Suffolk that if Lincolnshire caused any more trouble, he should 'destroy, burn and kill man, woman and child, to the terrible example of all others'.

But the flames of rebellion had spread. Reports of new disturbances were flooding in from across the North. And one name kept coming up: Robert Aske.

After parting company with the Lincolnshire rebels, Aske had intended to go back to his sister's house. But when he crossed the Humber into the rain-soaked marshlands of east Yorkshire, he found the villages there in uproar, too.

Aske's head was whirling. What should he do? Ignore them and go home? Try to calm their rising tempers?

But amid the fog of uncertainty, he heard that voice again in his head. He was an educated man. He agreed with everything the rebels wanted. He should lead them, and speak for England.

So he did. On 11 October, the new Chief Captain of the Marshland issued his first proclamation, urging local men to be ready to 'preserve the Church of God'.

More men rallied to his side. In Aske's words, they were not rebels, but 'pilgrims' for the true faith. So the rebellion got its name: the Pilgrimage of Grace.

By now civil war seemed a serious possibility. In London, Cromwell stared in horror at reports of rebel bands in Yorkshire, Lancashire, Cumberland and Westmorland, marching beneath saints' banners and holy relics.

On the 16th, Aske's men marched into York, for centuries the unofficial capital of northern England. There they swore an oath, pledging to defend the Catholic Church, root out the Protestant heretics and destroy the King's 'evil councillors'.

A few days later, the great castle at Pontefract surrendered without a fight. By this point, Aske was no longer merely the Chief Captain. Now he called himself the Grand Captain.

He was master of a third of England; yet just a week earlier, nobody had heard of him.

In London, rumours spread that the Emperor was about to send troops to the northerners' aid. Henry and Cromwell were so worried that they ordered their men to search every priest in the capital and to confiscate any weapon larger than a kitchen knife.

In the meantime, the Duke of Norfolk was approaching Yorkshire with some 8,000 troops. But as he neared Doncaster Bridge he could see the rebel host across the river: at least 30,000 of them, drawn up beneath the banners of Christ and the saints.

Norfolk knew these were impossible odds. So at the end of October, he proposed a truce.

Some of the boldest rebels urged Aske to ignore it. They would never have a better chance to smash the royal army, march to London and force their demands upon the King.

But at the crucial moment, the Grand Captain blinked. He had never seen himself as a disloyal man. So when Norfolk promised that Henry would give the rebels what they wanted, Aske desperately wanted to believe him.

Norfolk was lying, of course. In secret he told Henry to ignore 'whatever promises I shall make'. But in his innocence, Aske decided to trust him.

The next day the deal was done. There would be no battle. Instead, the rebels agreed to halt at the River Don, and send their demands to London.

Anyone who knew Henry could see their demands were completely unrealistic. The rebels wanted him to restore the Pope's authority, bring back the monasteries, recognize Mary as his true heir and send Cromwell to the chopping block. And, of course, they wanted a full pardon, too.

When Henry read them, he exploded with rage. There would be no Pope and no pardon. He would forgive them only if they handed over their ringleaders to be executed.

But then Norfolk intervened. It was much better, he murmured, to let the rebels think they had won. By soothing them with honeyed words, Henry could buy himself time to prepare.

And then, when he was ready, he could utterly destroy them.

Six weeks went by, heavy with tension. At last, at the beginning of December, a beaming Norfolk met the Grand Captain in the priory at Doncaster. He had good news, he said.

Henry agreed that a new Parliament would sort out the future of the English Church, and in the meantime he promised not to close down any more monasteries. And for the rebels there would be a free pardon, as long as they went home.

Some of the rebel captains hesitated. How could they trust a king who had broken so many promises? Wouldn't the Mouldwarp turn on them, as he had turned on his own wives?

But Aske had no doubts. Falling to his knees, he exclaimed that he was the Grand Captain no longer.

Reaching to his chest, he tore off the rebel symbol, the badge of Christ. He would 'now wear no badge nor sign', he said, 'but the badge of our sovereign lord' – the King.

And at first, it seemed that Aske was right. A week later, one of Henry's councillors brought him an extraordinary offer. To thank him for his loyalty, the King and Queen would like him to join them for Christmas.

It was an unusually cold winter, and as Londoners skated merrily over the frozen Thames, the Yorkshire lawyer arrived at Greenwich to find himself the man of the hour.

To his relief, Henry could hardly have been friendlier, while Jane was the soul of warmth and kindliness. There were no hard feelings, Henry said.

To show the people of the North how much he loved them, his next Parliament would meet in York. And Jane would be crowned Queen in York Minster, the first coronation in the city for almost five hundred years.

Tears of gratitude sprang to Aske's eyes. He had always hoped that the King would be generous, but this was wonderful! The true faith would return, the monasteries would be saved and England would be England once again.

On 5 January Aske said farewell to his hosts, and set off for the North with the good news. And as the Yorkshireman's horse disappeared into the distance, the smile faded from Henry's face.

Eleven days later, more trouble broke out in the North. And this gave Henry the excuse he needed.

Now he dropped the pretence of forgiveness. The northerners had broken the truce, so their pardons were cancelled. And since they had disbanded their army, there was nobody to shield them from their master's vengeance.

As Norfolk's troops marched into Yorkshire, Henry sent him bloodcurdling instructions. In 'every town, great or small', he wanted to see 'dreadful executions', without 'pity or respect'. He wanted a 'fearful spectacle' that the North would remember for the rest of time. And he got it.

In the next few weeks, more than two hundred people were slaughtered, many of them hanged, drawn and quartered. Rotting corpses hung from the trees; severed heads decorated the gates. The streets reeked of blood and fear. Henry had taught the North a lesson, all right.

And then there was Robert Aske.

As the North burned, Aske was numb with shock and confusion. When Henry ordered him to return to London, the voice in his head screamed that he should flee for his life.

But Aske did not listen. Henry was a good man. Surely he could be persuaded to stop the killing.

But when Aske arrived in London, there was no welcoming smile from Queen Jane. There were only the grim faces of the guards, who threw him into a cell in the Tower.

And there was no mercy for the Grand Captain. Sentenced to death for high treason, Aske was taken back to York under heavy guard.

On 12 July 1537, he was led onto the scaffold at York Castle, while a vast crowd watched below. There he was hanged in chains from the tower, his broken body twisting for hours in the wind: a horrifically slow, agonizing way to die.

Aske had paid the ultimate price for believing Henry's word. He had not been the first; and he would not be the last.

The defeat of the Pilgrimage of Grace was a colossal moment in England's history. If Aske and his friends had won, things might have taken a very different course. But their failure was a total disaster for the Catholic cause.

Now Cromwell had his chance to destroy the monasteries for ever. In the next few years, every last monastery, abbey, friary and nunnery was shut down. The monks were thrown out into the cold, their art collections carried off, their wealth transferred to the King.

In the Protestants' zeal to stamp out the old ways, cloisters were demolished, libraries destroyed, statues smashed to pieces. Sometimes Cromwell's men used explosives to blow up the ruins, so that only their ghosts would remain to haunt his new England.

For monks who tried to resist, there was no mercy. The Abbot of Colchester was hanged, drawn and quartered. So was the Abbot of Reading, whose body was displayed at his own gatehouse.

Then Cromwell turned to the ancient abbey at Glastonbury, wreathed in myth and mystery. Legend claimed that it was the last resting place of King Arthur, his tomb hidden beneath the high altar. But Cromwell wanted it destroyed.

In September 1539, his men arrived to search for treasure, which they found hidden in a secret vault. Then they questioned the abbot, Richard Whiting, who was almost eighty, 'very weak and sickly'.

Only a year earlier, Cromwell had assured him that he and his abbey were in no danger. But on 14 November the old man went on trial, charged with robbing his own church.

The verdict had already been decided. The next day, horses dragged him to the top of Glastonbury Tor, the hill overlooking the abbey.

There Whiting was hanged, drawn and quartered. Afterwards, his head was displayed above the old west gate of his own abbey.

But there was nobody to see it. The abbey had already been shut down.

For many people, the destruction of the monasteries came as a dreadful shock.

Even Jane felt she had to say something. According to the French ambassador, she 'threw herself on her knees before the King and begged him to restore the abbeys'.

Henry's face darkened. 'Get up!' he shouted. How often had he told her not to meddle with his affairs? It was for this sort of thing, he added menacingly, that his last queen had lost her head.

Jane got the message. She never mentioned the abbeys again.

By the spring of 1537, she had other things on her mind. At long last, after a year of marriage, she was expecting a child. Once again, Henry prayed for a son.

The summer passed, and the omens were good. In late September, Jane withdrew to the richly decorated apartments at Hampton Court. Tapestries were draped over the windows, and a cross hung above the bed.

The days went by, and the excitement grew. On the afternoon of 9 October Jane felt a lurch deep within her body. The time had come.

For two days, there was no news. At St Paul's Cathedral, the authorities organized a procession to 'pray for the Queen'. And then, at two in the morning on Friday, 12 October, the shrill cry of a newborn baby echoed down the corridors of Hampton Court.

It was a boy.

For Henry, now aged forty-six, it was a moment of

almost unimaginable triumph. When he took the squeal-ing red-faced infant in his arms, tears of joy ran down his face.

It had all been worth it, after all. At long last, a son, an heir, a future Tudor king!

The news spread quickly. Within hours, churches across the capital were offering prayers of thanksgiving. 'Thanks to our Lord God,' wrote the Protestant champion Hugh Latimer, 'for verily he hath showed himself God of England!'

That evening, bonfires blazed in the streets. The bells rang in patriotic celebration; the tables groaned with free food; excited crowds gathered around the barrels of wine.

Three days later, in the chapel at Hampton Court, Henry's heir was baptized by Archbishop Cranmer. He was christened Edward, harking back to the warrior kings of old.

Mary acted as the baby's godmother, and little Elizabeth helped to carry his white robe. Afterwards, Edward was car-ried back to his mother's apartment, where the exhausted Jane was propped up in bed, smiling with pride.

Something was not quite right, though. By the next morning, Jane was running a high fever, her brow hot to the touch, her clothes damp with sweat.

Everybody knew childbirth was risky. With no modern medicines to help them, thousands of women died from infection every year. Henry's own mother, Elizabeth of York, had died in childbirth when he was just eleven.

By Friday 19th, Jane's condition had worsened. At St Paul's, worshippers prayed for her recovery.

For a moment, she seemed to fight back. But by Tuesday evening she was sinking fast.

At dawn her chaplain arrived to pray with her for the last time. And just before midnight on Wednesday, 24 October, Jane's breathing slowed, faltered and faded into silence.

The girl from Wolf Hall, so kind and gentle, was dead. She was only twenty-eight, and had been married for less than two years.

Across the land, the cheers of celebration gave way to tears of grief. Down came the banners of joy; up went the black cloth of mourning.

After just twelve days, little Edward had lost his mother. For the third time, England had lost its queen. And once again, Henry was looking for a wife.

Henry VIII

PART FOUR

ANNE OF CLEVES

15

The Princess of Cleves

For Henry, Jane's death came as a shattering blow.

She had been so sweet, so gentle, so popular. She had given him the son he so desperately wanted. And now, through the cruellest twist of fate imaginable, she was gone.

For three months Henry grieved. Christmas came, dull and cheerless. Even little Edward, a healthy, bouncing boy, failed to lift his spirits.

At last, in February 1538, Henry put away his black mourning clothes and turned his mind to the future. And as always, it came down to the same old question. Whom should he marry next?

He could, of course, have married nobody. But the court needed a queen, and Henry himself was not yet fifty. He wanted a wife, and he wanted more sons.

But there was another, perhaps even more important reason. A royal marriage meant an alliance – and if there was one thing England desperately needed, it was a reliable ally.

Henry's break with Rome had left him dangerously

isolated. For a time, he and Cromwell reassured themselves that the Emperor Charles and King Francis were too busy fighting each other to think about England.

But that summer, terrible news arrived from the south of France. In the city of Nice, the Pope had arranged a ten-year truce between France and the Holy Roman Empire.

After years of bloody fighting, the two greatest powers in Europe were now friends, which meant their eyes were bound to fall on England.

Worse was to follow.

On 17 December, the Pope issued a dramatic decree kicking Henry out of the Christian family. In the eyes of Rome, Henry was not just an outlaw, he was the servant of the Devil.

One day, he would burn in hell. But now the Pope urged Charles and Francis to launch a crusade against the English tyrant as soon as possible.

Never had England stood in greater danger. From Whitehall, Henry sent urgent orders across the country. Soldiers and sailors must be drilled and mustered, arms and armour must be polished and prepared.

In the shipyards, men worked around the clock to re-inforce the Channel fleet. On the clifftops along the south coast, construction crews hurried to build castles, beacons, forts and gun platforms.*

---

* Many of these splendid buildings are still standing today, such as Pendennis Castle in Cornwall and Walmer Castle in Kent, and are well worth a visit.

For Henry, these were the darkest of days. But never did he consider backing down.

Not long after the Pope's call to arms, Cromwell organized a spectacular demonstration of England's defiance. While huge crowds watched on the banks of the Thames, two barges rowed back and forth.

One was decorated with Henry's colours. On the other, men dressed as the Pope and his cardinals waved their arms furiously in the air.

All the time, guns on the two boats blazed away, although they were only firing blanks. At last Henry's boat was victorious, and the Pope was hurled spluttering into the Thames.

It was all tremendous fun, and on the bank Henry cheered louder than anybody. But he knew only too well that if his enemies attacked, it would take more than a couple of barges to stop them.

In his City townhouse, Cromwell sat alone, lost in thought.

After the King himself, he was the most powerful man in England. His agents were everywhere. The monasteries were in ruins; the Catholics were in retreat.

But Cromwell had seen the wheel turn too many times

to think he was invincible. He knew he had plenty of enemies at court, especially among the old nobility.

And he knew all his success depended on Henry's favour. If the King changed his mind, everything Cromwell had built could collapse in an instant. So if Henry wanted a new wife, Cromwell simply *had* to get it right.

Any new bride had to be young enough to have children. She also had to be pretty, because Henry was hard to please.

But at the same time, Cromwell had to think about the bigger picture. Ideally, the new queen would come from a country that would help England against the Emperor.

In the first months after Jane's death, there was talk of Henry marrying a princess from France. Henry himself rather liked the idea.

Talking to the French ambassador, he suggested that King Francis should send seven or eight candidates to Calais. He would then cross the Channel, the girls could put on a beauty parade, and he would choose the most attractive to take home.

The ambassador's eyes widened in disbelief. Perhaps Henry would like to try kissing them all first? 'Is that,' he asked sarcastically, 'the way the Knights of the Round Table treated women in your country in times past?'

At that, even Henry turned red, and gave an embarrassed laugh.

But when Cromwell thought about it, the French idea seemed a non-starter. They were never going to get an alliance with King Francis, so what was the point?

For hours he studied the European chessboard, weighing up the possible alliances. And again and again his eye was drawn to a small but strategically vital state on the Holy Roman Empire's northern fringe – the Duchy of Cleves.

Straddling the border between modern-day Germany and Holland, Cleves had managed to escape the fighting between Lutherans and Catholics, who were tearing the rest of Germany apart.

But old Duke John was very friendly with Germany's Protestant rulers. So if Henry and Cromwell could win him over, they might strike an alliance with the Protestant League of German states.

And as luck would have it, the Duke had a daughter.

Some three hundred miles to the east, in the great island castle at Düren, a young woman sat with her ladies in a companionable silence, bent over her needle and thread.

In the summer of 1538, Anne of Cleves was twenty-three years old. Cleves was a jolly, boisterous place, its people famously fond of their local beer. But Anne's parents had brought her up to be good – and she was.

Quiet and unassuming, Anne had never learned any language but her native German. She had never been taught to sing, and could not play an instrument. She spent her days sewing in her chamber, protected from the harsh realities of the outside world.

Nothing in Anne's life had prepared her for the plots and snares of the English court. But when Henry's ambassador arrived in Cleves, he thought all the signs were good.

Everybody spoke highly of Anne's kindness and modesty. And although the ambassador had only glimpsed her in a cloak and hood, everybody said she was very pretty.

This all sounded splendid, and by the following spring Henry's envoys had opened talks with the Duke for his daughter's hand. Still, it made sense to be sure. So that August, Henry asked his favourite artist, Hans Holbein, to go to Cleves and paint Anne's portrait.

Off Holbein went to Düren, where he spent a week painting the young princess. He got back to England at the end of the summer and carefully unveiled the canvas. And at once a smile spread over Henry's features.

The portrait showed a serious, thoughtful young woman, with brown eyes, a broad forehead and a slightly wide nose. Was Anne one of Europe's great beauties? Perhaps not, but she had nothing to be ashamed of, either.

All was well, then, and Henry gave Cromwell the go-ahead. Within weeks the deal was done, and as the autumn drizzle began to fall, Anne packed her bags and said farewell to her parents.

It was almost forty years since another foreign princess, Catherine of Aragon, had made the long journey to

England. Now Anne and her servants rode west, through Düsseldorf, Cleves and Antwerp.

By mid-December she had reached the port of Calais, an English stronghold for two centuries. Winter had brought howling gales and driving rain, so here she halted for a couple of weeks.

Once again the reports were excellent. In her letters home, the governor's wife wrote that Anne was 'good and gentle to serve and please'. Everybody liked her, and Henry was bound to be delighted with his bride.

On 27 December, the winds eased. At Calais, Anne boarded the royal flagship, its flags and pennants fluttering in the breeze. And as the church bells tolled seven that evening, the Princess of Cleves stepped onto the soil of her new country.

The weather was awful, with hail blowing into Anne's face, and it took hours to unload her belongings from the ship. But as the welcoming party reported to Henry, she remained as patient as ever, a model of queenly dignity.

By the last day of 1539, Anne had reached Rochester, where she was to stay at the Bishop's Palace. She was still in good spirits, if a little weary after such a long journey.

And it was there, the following day, that things went catastrophically wrong.

It was afternoon on New Year's Day, and the winter sun was dipping towards the horizon.

At the Bishop's Palace, Anne stood at the window. Down below the locals had put on a bull-baiting show. But her mind was hundreds of miles away, with her friends and family back in Cleves.

Suddenly footsteps sounded on the stairs, and a man appeared in the doorway, panting for breath.

Sir Anthony Browne, Master of the King's Horse, had left Greenwich earlier that day. The King was bored with waiting for his young bride, and had decided to welcome her with a grand, romantic gesture.

To cut a long story short, Henry had ridden to Rochester to surprise her. In what he considered a hilarious prank, he and his friends were wearing identical multi-coloured hoods and capes, like Robin Hood and his Merry Men.

Out of politeness, Henry had sent Browne ahead to warn his future wife. But now, as Browne gasped out his explanation, the words died on his lips.

For Anne did not find the idea funny. She just stared at him, frowning in bewilderment, as if she had never heard of anything like it.

At that moment, Browne knew she was wrong for Henry. She was far, far too serious. He had, he later recalled, never been 'more dismayed in all his life'.

But it was too late to warn his master, for already he could hear people running up the stairs. The door burst open, and three men in multi-coloured hoods leaped into the room, roaring with laughter.

Anne said nothing. She glanced in bewilderment at her German ladies, and gave a nervous half-smile.

The largest of the newcomers bowed low and held out a gift. It was a present for the princess, he said grandly, from the King himself.

Baffled, Anne took the gift. Then she turned back to watch the bull-baiting.

The stranger said something. Anne shot him a tired glance, muttered in German and turned back to the window.

There was a long, dreadful silence. The large man stood there, completely flummoxed. Then, clearly frustrated, he strode out of the room.

A few moments later he returned, this time without his hood, dressed in a magnificent purple robe. Only now did Anne realize that he was her future husband.

She tried to smile, but it was too late. Henry could barely bring himself to look her in the eye.

He asked a few questions about her journey. Then, as soon as it was polite to do so, he made his excuses and left.

Henry's friends had never seen him so embarrassed. On the barge back to Greenwich he sulked in silence. Finally he roused himself and called for Browne.

'I see nothing in this woman as men report of her,' Henry said bitterly. 'And I marvel that men would make such report as they have done.'

Browne said nothing. What was there to say?

Then Henry turned to another friend, Sir John Russell: 'How like you this woman? Do you think her so fair and of such beauty as has been reported to me?'

Russell stammered something about Anne looking a bit browner than he had expected. Henry shook his head. 'Alas!' he muttered. 'Whom should men trust?'

She was *nothing* like her portrait, he said bitterly. 'I like her not.'

At Greenwich, Cromwell was waiting. 'How did you like the Lady Anne?' he asked. Then he saw the King's expression, and the smile faded from his face.

'Nothing so well as she was spoken of,' Henry said grimly. If he had known what she was really like, 'she should not have come within this realm'.

Then, as if musing aloud, he murmured: 'What remedy?'

Cromwell stood frozen with horror. For once, his mind was blank. The deal was done. They could not go back on it now.

'I am very sorry,' he said limply. 'I know none.'

Two days later, Anne arrived at Greenwich. When she was safely installed in her apartments, Henry went to find Cromwell.

'Well?' he asked. 'Is it not as I told you? Say what they will, she is nothing as fair as hath been reported.'

Usually so cool and unreadable, Cromwell seemed lost for words. Anne had a very 'queenly manner', he said finally. But he could see his master was not happy at all.

The marriage was supposed to take place the next day, but Henry put it off. Instead, while a bewildered Anne waited in her apartments, his councillors pored over the details of the deal. But there was no way out.

When Cromwell delivered the bad news, Henry shook his head. 'I am not well handled,' he said darkly. If it were not for his fear of driving 'her brother into the hands of the Emperor', he would never dream of marrying her.

'Is there none other remedy,' he asked, 'but that I must, against my will, put my neck into the yoke?'

Again Cromwell spread his hands helplessly, and said nothing.

So on the morning of Tuesday, 6 January, Henry trudged down the gallery of Greenwich Palace. Passing Cromwell, he shook his head. 'My Lord,' Henry muttered grumpily, 'if it were not to satisfy the world, and my realm, I would not do that which I must do this day.'

Cromwell gave a pained half-smile, and tried to tell himself that the King would come around to the German girl eventually.

Now Anne appeared, magnificently dressed in a long, pearl-encrusted gown. Her fair hair fell long and free, and on her head she wore a coronet of gold, with sprigs of rosemary.

She made three deep curtseys, and then Henry led her into the chamber where Archbishop Cranmer waited.

The service did not take long. Soon the ring, engraved with the words 'God Send Me Well to Keep', was on Anne's finger, and they were husband and wife.

The rest of the day passed in a blur of drinking and dancing. Henry had seen it all before. For Anne, though, everything was new.

Only a few weeks earlier she had been at home in Cleves, sewing with her friends. Now she was Queen of a strange country where she barely spoke the language.

As always, she seemed the soul of dignity. The conversation flowed around her, and she just sat there, smiling vaguely, as calm and serious as ever.

Darkness fell. The King and Queen made their way to the bridal chamber. The door closed. Henry blew out the candle. And before long the happy couple were fast asleep.

The next morning, Cromwell came into the royal apartments to find his master already there, with a face like thunder.

'How liked you the Queen?' Cromwell asked, trying to sound cheerful.

Henry shook his head. 'As ye know,' he said grimly, 'I liked her before not well, but now I like her much worse.'

Cromwell nodded. His face gave nothing away, but his spirits could hardly have been lower.

Later that morning, Henry talked to his doctors. He could not stand the Queen, he said frankly. He found her so unattractive he could barely kiss her.

Unless something changed, there was clearly little chance of Henry and Anne settling down and starting a family. His doctors furrowed their brows, but there was not much they could do about it.

The odd thing was that nobody else could see anything wrong with Anne. It was true that she was very serious, but she was not ugly.

So what on earth was wrong? Why had he taken such a violent dislike to her?

Perhaps the answer was this. Deep down, beneath the layers of fat, Henry was still a boyish romantic. He saw himself as a hero of legend, and dreamed of having a stylish, graceful queen, who doted on his every word.

But Anne of Cleves was not stylish. She was not exotic and sophisticated, as Catherine had been; or sharp and clever, like Anne Boleyn; or gentle and sweet-natured, like Jane.

No minstrel would ever write a song about her. No knight would ever swoon at her feet. She was bland. She was boring. She was German.

So the weeks went by. Every evening Henry kissed Anne goodnight, and went straight to sleep. Every morning he kissed her again, and made a hasty exit. Apart from that, they barely spoke at all.

Meanwhile, Cromwell's mind was elsewhere. The threat of invasion had faded, thank goodness, but there was so much else to do: monasteries and nunneries, Bibles and bridges, Church regulations and coastal defences.

His spies reported a rumour that Henry had fallen in love again, this time with some little niece of the Duke of Norfolk. But Cromwell gave it scant thought. If Henry had somebody to distract him from the German girl, then so much the better.

The days lengthened. The wild flowers bloomed. The birds sang in the orchards and hedgerows.

On 17 April Cromwell was named Earl of Essex, an astonishing achievement for a humble brewer's son. The next day, Henry made him Lord Great Chamberlain. And five days after that, he became a Knight of the Garter, joining the highest order of chivalry in the land.

Never had Cromwell's star been higher. More than ever before, he seemed a man who could do no wrong, the master of all he surveyed.

And then, just a few weeks later, it all came crashing down.

PART FIVE

CATHERINE HOWARD

16

To the Tower!

The girl's name was Catherine Howard. She was about eighteen, very short and very pretty, with sparkling eyes.

Nobody was quite sure when Henry noticed her. But later, some people remembered the Bishop of Winchester's feast in March, when she had danced in the rose-tinted light of the great stained-glass window.

Perhaps it was that evening, they said, that the King had fallen head over heels in love, even though she was six years younger than his elder daughter.

What was it about Catherine Howard that caught his attention? She was good-looking, certainly. But there was more to it than that.

The contrast with his wife could hardly have been starker. Anne was serious, solemn and ever so slightly disapproving.

But when Catherine's face lit up with that infectious grin, you knew she liked a good time. She was charming. She was funny. She was *fun*.

She had only been at court for a few months, having

arrived to attend the new Queen. Like Anne Boleyn, she belonged to the rich and powerful Norfolk clan. The ruthless Duke, whose soldiers had wreaked such havoc in the North, was her uncle, too.

But her mother had died when she was young, and her father had married again and gone off to Calais. So Catherine had spent her teenage years living with her grandmother, Agnes Howard, at her Sussex manor house.

Life in her grandmother's household was not exactly strict. Catherine was one of several Howard girls who slept in the Maidens' Chamber, two to a bed, as if it were a boarding-school dormitory.

They served as her grandmother's ladies-in-waiting, but they also learned the skills expected of princesses. The secretaries taught them to read and write, and a music teacher taught them to sing and play.

The atmosphere, though, was giddier than in any boarding school. When Catherine was about fifteen, her grandmother caught her kissing the music teacher, a young man called Henry Mannox, and gave her two hard smacks on the head.

A year or so later, Catherine acquired a new boyfriend. This was another Howard relative, a young man called Francis Dereham, who was staying at her grandmother's other house in Lambeth, on the south bank of the Thames.

According to family gossip, Catherine persuaded her grandmother's maid to steal the key to the Maidens' Chamber, which was usually locked at night. Then, after lights out, Catherine unlocked the door, allowing Dereham and his friends to sneak in for secret parties.

Every night the young men smuggled in wine, strawberries and other treats, and they settled down to a midnight feast, with all sorts of kissing and tickling. This was strictly against the rules, but Catherine was sure they would get away with it.

Unfortunately, she had not bargained on Henry Mannox. The music teacher was hurt to have been left out of the midnight parties, and as the weeks went by he became more and more jealous.

Eventually Mannox scribbled an anonymous letter to Catherine's grandmother, which he left on her seat before church. Catherine duly got into trouble, and afterwards Dereham and Mannox almost came to blows.

Still, it was not the end of the world. Catherine was naughty, but she was a teenager, not a saint. So what if she sometimes broke the rules?

Catherine moved to Greenwich Palace at the turn of 1540. The Howards had better connections than any family in England, and her grandmother had managed to get her a position as one of the new Queen's ladies-in-waiting.

Never in their wildest dreams had any of the Howards imagined that little Catherine would catch the eye of the King. But when they noticed him looking at her, they seized their opportunity.

The head of the family, the Duke of Norfolk, had always been loyal to Henry. But over the years he had become deeply suspicious of the new religion. Like many of the old noblemen, he was a Catholic, and he hated the thought of change.

Even more importantly, Norfolk was intensely jealous of Cromwell. A man of towering, haughty pride, he dreamed of forcing Cromwell out and becoming the main player at court.

So when he heard that the King had developed a fancy for another of his nieces, he rubbed his hands with glee.

All talk of Catherine's previous boyfriends was hurriedly brushed under the carpet. Norfolk knew Henry liked his sweethearts to be perfect, so Catherine must be perfect, too.

The young girl was secretly drilled in 'how to behave to the King'. Her grandmother taught her when to smile and when to curtsey, how to make Henry laugh and how to keep him interested. And Norfolk's friends organized lots of dinners and parties, where Catherine and Henry could be brought together as much as possible.

It worked. By late spring, the King was smitten. After the shock of Jane's death and the crushing disappointment of his German marriage, he felt young, alive, reborn in the thrill of the chase.

Just as he had pursued Anne Boleyn and Jane Seymour,

now he wooed Catherine Howard. She was, he declared, his 'blushing rose without a thorn'. He simply could not live without her.

In the darkness, Norfolk watched and waited, a smirk playing on his lips. Out of nowhere, fate had handed him a deadly weapon. Now he proposed to use it.

It was the afternoon of Thursday, 10 June, a bright, breezy summer's day.

Thomas Cromwell had spent the morning at Westminster, listening to the debates in the House of Lords. As Earl of Essex, he was dressed in his nobleman's finery, the Order of St George glittering on his breast, the Garter tied around his leg.

Afterwards Cromwell went to the palace, as usual, to have lunch with his fellow councillors. If he had been less distracted, he might have noticed that they looked away when he sat down, and that none of them addressed a single remark to him.

But he was preoccupied with work. In Calais, some of his Protestant friends had been accused of heresy. The King was concerned that the religious revolution was going too far, so Cromwell had to be careful.

Abroad, the European picture was shifting rapidly, with reports of a new feud between France and the Empire. And then there were these rumours about the Howard girl. He really ought to look into that before it got out of hand . . .

After lunch, the councillors went upstairs for their regular meeting. Cromwell followed on later, as he usually did, and by the time he got to the council chamber the others were already in their places.

It was when he reached for his chair that Norfolk spoke: 'Cromwell, do not sit there! Traitors do not sit amongst gentlemen!'

For a moment, Cromwell could not believe his ears. 'I am not a traitor!' he shot back indignantly. But already the Captain of the Guard was at his side, a hand on his arm.

'I arrest you,' the captain said, rather unnecessarily.

'What for?' Cromwell snapped.

'That you will learn elsewhere,' the captain said.

Now Cromwell was like a cornered animal. His face scarlet with anger, his voice almost breaking in desperation, he threw his cap on the floor in rage. He was no traitor, and they knew it! The King would protect him! Let him speak to the King!

Tightening his grip, the captain tried to pull him away. 'Stop, captain,' Norfolk said.

He reached for the badge of St George around Cromwell's neck, and ripped it off. Meanwhile the Earl of Southampton was tearing off the Garter.

'Traitors must not wear the Garter,' Norfolk snarled.

It was useless to resist. There were too many of them, and too many guards at the captain's back.

A few moments later, with the hisses of 'Traitor!' ringing in his ears, Cromwell stumbled down the back stairs towards the river. The barge was already there, waiting unobserved.

The journey to the Tower did not take long. As night fell, the most powerful politician in England was behind bars, still loudly protesting that he was no traitor and had done nothing wrong.

Already soldiers had sealed off his City townhouse and were making lists of all his belongings. His treasures, his money, even his crockery and plates, were stacked up and loaded into crates, just like his friend Wolsey's, all those years ago.

When Henry had finished with you, he took everything. Those were the rules of the game.

For eighteen days, Cromwell remained in the Tower. At first, hoping against hope, he pleaded to see the King, convinced that there must have been some mistake.

In desperation he scribbled letter after letter. He begged Henry to remember the 'labours and pains' he had taken on his behalf. He called himself Henry's 'most miserable prisoner and poor slave'.

He claimed that he looked to Henry as a 'dear father', not as a master. And at last, in his fear and anguish, he yielded to panic: 'Most gracious prince, I cry for mercy, mercy, mercy!'

But deep down, in the darkest part of his soul, Cromwell knew it was all over. He had seen similar things happen to Wolsey, and to More, and to so many others. Even Anne Boleyn had not escaped. Why would he be any different?

There would be no trial. Henry did not want his most private secrets aired in public.

Instead, at the end of June, Parliament condemned the former Secretary for taking bribes, encouraging 'damnable errors and heresies' and plotting to marry the Lady Mary. He was 'the most false and corrupt traitor, deceiver and circumventor . . . that had ever been known'.

Almost none of it was true, but that hardly mattered. The wheel had turned, and Cromwell had fallen. It was a very familiar story.

The guards came for him on the morning of 28 July. By then, Cromwell was ready.

True to form, he walked to the scaffold with no signs of fear. His face a mask of self-control, he told the crowd that he died in the faith of the true Church.

He placed his trust, he said, in the 'merciful goodness' of Christ. And with a wry, mocking half-smile, he prayed for the life of the King, and his fellow councillors.

Cromwell knelt, and put his head on the block. The executioner lifted the axe, and the game was over.

That same day, at a country house in Surrey, Henry married Catherine Howard.

In the meantime, what on earth had happened to poor Anne of Cleves?

All spring, Anne had remained completely in the dark. She had been too busy learning English, and getting used to life in her new country, to notice that her husband had become besotted with her teenage lady-in-waiting.

But by the middle of June, Anne had finally realized that something strange was happening. Her attendants brought news of a tremendous argument in the council, and she could not help noticing that Cromwell had disappeared.

On 24 June, a messenger arrived from her husband. There was plague in the city, he said. For her own good, Anne should move out to Richmond for the time being.

With a heavy heart, Anne agreed. Deep down, she knew something was wrong.

Two weeks later, more news came. As usual, Henry did not have the courage to deliver it himself, but sent his councillors to do it for him.

When they told Anne that the Church of England was investigating her marriage, she managed to keep her composure. Surely this was all a mistake and would soon be sorted out?

But on Saturday, 10 July, another messenger brought a formal request that she agree to a divorce. And now Anne's defences gave way. She burst into tears, almost fainting with shock and shame.

It was an awful scene. 'Good Lord,' wrote the ambassador from Cleves, who tried to comfort her, 'she made such tears and bitter cries, it would break a heart of stone.'

That night, Anne sobbed herself to sleep. But by the time she woke, her mind was clear. In her quiet, understated way, the Princess of Cleves was as tough as anybody.

Henry wanted her gone. Fine. He was fat and old, and she would not miss him. But she was going to get something out of it.

In the next few days, Henry put together an offer. He promised that once the divorce went through, Anne would be treated as his 'good sister'. After the new Queen and his daughters, she would be ranked as the first lady in England.

She could have two palaces, at Richmond and Bletchingley, as well as several manors and estates. She was welcome to visit the court whenever she wanted, and would always be treated honourably.

She could keep all her fine clothes, her jewels and her servants. She would have her own household and her own cook. And above all, she would get some £4,000 a year, the equivalent of tens of millions of pounds today.

This was a spectacularly good deal by any standards. The only condition was that Anne must stay in England, and could never 'pass beyond the sea' while Henry was alive.

So the choice was clear. She could go back to Cleves, rejected and humiliated, to make a new marriage with some second-division German count. Or she could stay in England, with two palaces, buckets of money and nobody to tell her what to do.

It did not take her long to make up her mind. A few days later, she wrote home to Cleves with the news that after just six months, her marriage was over. But, she said, she was going to stay in England anyway.

Then, in good sensible German style, she sat down and ate a hearty dinner. And after that she asked a messenger to return her wedding ring to the King, 'desiring that it might be broken in pieces as a thing which she knew of no force or value'.

And with that, Anne of Cleves went contentedly to bed.

To many people, these new turns of the wheel were simply beyond belief. When King Francis heard that his English rival had executed his chief minister and got rid of yet another queen, he shook his head incredulously.

'The Queen that now is?' he asked, just to be sure. Then he gave a long sigh of amazement: 'Ah!'

In England it was a punishingly hot summer. For almost four months, no rain fell at all. In the fields, cows and sheep died where they stood. The sweating sickness was abroad again, and bodies piled up in the 'plague pits' outside major towns.

But Henry had never been happier. Overjoyed with his new bride, he began every day with a new spring in his step.

Determined to lose weight and impress his young wife, he got up every morning before six, went to church and then went hunting. He felt like a new man, and the age gap did not bother him one bit.

To most observers, the King seemed utterly besotted, like a boy with his first girlfriend. As for Catherine, she was walking on air – and with good reason.

She was the Queen, with more diamonds, pearls, emeralds and rubies than she had ever imagined. Men bowed to her; women curtsied wherever she went.

There was only one small cloud in the sky. The Lady Mary did not approve of her father's teenage bride at all, and treated her with scarcely veiled disdain.

It was true that Catherine was not highly educated. She once remarked that she was reluctant to confess her sins in church – *any* church – because her husband was Supreme Head of the Church, which meant he could hear everything. Even her admirers thought that was a bit dim.

But she was so young, so pretty, so full of life that few

people seriously disliked her. And as the months went by, Henry's ardour showed no signs of fading.

On New Year's Day he presented Catherine with yet more jewels – which went down rather better than the present he had taken to his last wife at Rochester a year earlier.

Two days later a visitor arrived at Hampton Court. It was Anne of Cleves, paying her first call on the royal couple since the high drama of the summer. And to everybody's surprise, it went remarkably well.

On arrival, Anne made a great show of kneeling before the new Queen, even though Catherine had been her lady-in-waiting only a few months earlier. At once Catherine asked her to rise, and showed her 'great favour and courtesy'.

Even Henry was on his best behaviour. Greeting Anne like a long-lost relative, he embraced and kissed her before inviting her to join them for supper.

The three of them sat down to a very cheerful meal, chattering away like old friends. And when Henry retired to bed, the two young women called for music, and spent a jolly evening dancing with a couple of courtiers.

All was well, then, at the royal court. Catherine was happy. Anne was happy. And for once, even Henry was happy.

The hatreds of the past had been forgotten. The days of plotting and feuding were over. And England could look forward to a new golden age, with its pretty, fun-loving young queen.

It didn't last long, though.

17

A Conspiracy Unmasked

In the summer of 1541, Henry and Catherine went on a trip.

The King often left London during the summer, partly to escape the plague, but also to get away from the stench of the open sewers. And this time, he had planned something special.

At long last, he was going north. There had been more trouble in Yorkshire, and he was determined to dazzle his northern subjects with his magnificence and might.

At the end of June, the royal couple rode out of London. And almost six weeks later, after a painfully slow journey through driving rain and muddy countryside, they reached the city of Lincoln.

Seven miles outside the city the long procession of councillors and courtiers, carts and baggage finally came to a halt. Here, their advance guard had put up three huge tents and laid out a picnic. And here, Lincoln's mayor was waiting, with handsome presents and grovelling apologies for the city's role in Robert Aske's rebellion.

After Henry and Catherine had rested, they got changed, exchanging their velvet travelling gear for shimmering robes of gold and silver. Then they rode into the city.

As the long train of horses and carriages came into view, the trumpets blared, the drums rolled and the crowds cheered. It was the kind of public spectacle Lincoln had not seen for years – a glittering reminder of Tudor splendour.

As the procession reached the cathedral, they halted once again. The King and Queen dismounted and knelt on a gorgeous carpet. Now the bishop appeared, wreathed in incense, dressed in his multi-coloured finery and carrying a golden cross for them to kiss.

As the voices of the choir soared towards the heavens, Henry and Catherine rose and walked together towards the altar to pray for God's blessing.

That night, as the royal couple feasted on roast venison, Lincoln celebrated. For the townsfolk, this had been a rare chance to catch a glimpse of their king, and the alehouses were buzzing with excitement.

How tall he was, and how elegantly dressed! Such wealth! Such majesty! And the Queen – how tiny she was, how young and how pretty!

Darkness fell. The lights gleamed in the tavern windows. Laughter drifted through the shadowed streets.

In the Bishop's Palace, the servants were clearing away the remains of the feast. The candles were burning low. Upstairs, the King and Queen had retired to bed.

Behind the door of Henry's bedchamber, all was darkness. Only the sound of snoring broke the silence.

But through the keyhole of Catherine's door, there came a tiny chink of light. Every now and again, there was the faint sound of movement, a hint of muffled giggling. Catherine and her lady-in-waiting must be up to something – but what?

Outside, the night watchman was doing his rounds. As he turned the corner of the Bishop's Palace, he passed a little door, the kind of door you might easily overlook.

Behind it were the secret back stairs, which led right up to the Queen's apartments. And as the watchman raised his light, he noticed something strange. *The door was ajar.*

Frowning, the watchman pulled the door shut and locked it. Then he disappeared around the corner, into the night.

A moment later, another man stepped out of the shadows, a thin smirk playing on his lips. For a moment his hands were busy at the lock. The door clicked open.

With a last, quick look around him, the stranger slipped through the doorway, and was gone.

Henry and Catherine did not return to Hampton Court until the end of October, in time for the feast of All Souls.

They were in excellent spirits. The tour of the North had

been a triumph. Henry's subjects had been suitably remorseful, the King had been cheered on every side, and his pretty young wife had captured hearts wherever she went.

Never had Catherine seemed so radiant. Never had Henry been prouder of his bride.

A few days before they got home, he presented her with a dazzling golden brooch, inlaid with diamonds and rubies. It was the ideal gift, he said, for a perfect wife, a model of 'virtue and good behaviour'.

All Souls' Day, 2 November, dawned cool and bright. In the gilded chapel at Hampton Court, the priests were lighting the candles for the service in remembrance of the dead.

If they had only looked up, they might have noticed a robed figure stealing into the royal box, which looked down on the chapel. From his gown he took a note and slipped it onto the King's seat. A moment later he was gone.

An hour later, when Henry made his way into the box for the service, he found the letter. But he did not read it until afterwards, when he was back in his private chamber.

And when he did, the blood drained from his features.

The robed man was Archbishop Cranmer. In plain, unflinching terms, his letter told the King that Catherine had lied to him about her life before her marriage, and might still be lying to him now.

Henry could not believe it. Catherine, his jewel of womanhood, a liar? Never!

He summoned his guards. Where was Cranmer?

A few moments later, the Archbishop appeared in the doorway, wringing his hands. It was all true, he said sadly.

While the royal couple were away in the North, Cranmer had received a visit from a courtier called John Lascelles. A fervent Protestant who had once worked for Thomas Cromwell, Lascelles hated the Howards and was determined to get revenge for his old master's fall.

As luck would have it, Lascelles's sister Mary worked for Catherine's grandmother, old Agnes Howard. She knew all the gossip about the teenage Catherine, and had passed it on to her brother. Lascelles told it to Cranmer; and now Cranmer relayed it to the King.

So what were these terrible secrets?

Lascelles had discovered the story about Catherine and her music teacher, Henry Mannox. He also passed on the tales of her midnight parties with Francis Dereham, and suggested that she had promised to marry Dereham one day.

In themselves, these stories were not really so bad. The problem, though, was that Catherine and her family had covered them up. They had presented her as the picture of perfection, a lily-white maiden who had never had a boy-friend and would never dream of breaking the rules.

To Henry, so fearful of plots and conspiracies, all this was deeply disturbing. Yet at first he sprang to Catherine's defence. The stories must be forgeries, because his beloved wife would never lie to him.

All the same, he agreed that they should be investigated. He would ask four of his closest councillors to make enquiries, so that Catherine could be cleared of 'any spark of scandal'.

That night, Henry set the machinery in motion. And three days later, on the evening of Saturday, 5 November, the councillors reported their findings.

As Henry listened, his eyes hardened.

His councillors had spoken to Lascelles's sister Mary, and she had stuck to her story. Then they had questioned the music teacher, Mannox, and he admitted it was true. He claimed that he and Catherine had been in love, but Dereham had stolen her from him.

Next they had spoken to Catherine's old friends, who said they had seen her and Dereham kissing like 'two sparrows'. And finally they had interrogated Dereham himself. He admitted sneaking into Catherine's room, and even into her bed.

There was more, the councillors added. Although Catherine and Dereham had parted company when she moved to court, he had since come back into her life.

Late that summer, during the trip to the North, she had appointed Dereham as her private secretary. At the time, nobody had thought anything of it. But in the light of these revelations, it looked very suspicious.

The councillors stopped, and looked up. Henry was crying. Tears rolled down his fat cheeks.

Then he roused himself. There was no point in weeping. It was time for action.

In secret, messages went out to his senior councillors. The King wanted to see them on Sunday evening, at Whitehall.

The following morning, Henry left Hampton Court early to go hunting. Catherine spent the day practising her dancing steps with her ladies.

Her husband's departure was nothing unusual, and she thought little of it. But she would never lay eyes on him again.

The meeting began late on Sunday, as the bells were tolling midnight. All the major figures were there: even Catherine's uncle, the Duke of Norfolk, his face cold and set.

Once again, the four councillors laid out the evidence, in painstaking, excruciating detail. And now something extraordinary happened.

Having opened the meeting with icy self-control, Henry burst into floods of tears, ranting and raving like a madman. It was his councillors who had persuaded him to marry this 'wicked woman'. They *must* have known! They had lied to him, tricked him, made a fool of him!

His face contorted with rage, his voice broken by sobs, Henry went on and on. Catherine must pay for humiliating him. If he had a sword, he would kill her on the spot. She would die slowly, in unspeakable agony!

Gradually his anger burned itself out, and turned into whimpering self-pity. Why, why, he cried, had God tormented him with 'such ill-conditioned wives'?

Henry's voice tailed off. The councillors glanced anxiously at one another. Somebody, clearly, was going to have to talk to the Queen.

A few hours later, guards sealed off Catherine's chambers. When the musicians arrived for her dancing practice, they found the doors barred. 'There is no more time to dance,' one of the guards said coldly.

That evening, Cranmer rode to Hampton Court. Almost alone among Henry's senior advisers, the Archbishop was not a hard man. He understood human frailty, and his voice was patient and kind.

At first, Catherine made a feeble attempt to deny everything. But as Cranmer probed, her resistance collapsed and she broke down in tears.

It was true, she sobbed. But she had been so 'blinded with desire of worldly glory' that she had never stopped to think what a crime it was, to hide her 'former faults' from her husband.

Afterwards, Cranmer told Henry he had never seen anybody so stricken with guilt and terror. 'It would have pitied any man's heart in the world,' he said sadly, 'to have looked upon her.'

Henry nodded. His rage had died down now, and he had been thinking.

Catherine was still very young. Perhaps she had never meant to deceive him, so he had decided to be merciful.

Instead of being sent to the Tower, Catherine would be moved to the old abbey at Syon, on the bank of the Thames. She would be confined to a small apartment, with six of her favourite dresses and four ladies-in-waiting. There she would stay, until Henry had decided what to do.

On 11 November, Cranmer relayed this information to the Queen, and Catherine gave a long, shuddering sigh of relief. She was not going to die, after all. How merciful her husband was! What a 'gracious and loving prince'!

But there was a twist.

At that very moment, in the Tower of London, Francis Dereham was pleading desperately for his life. The guards were convinced he was hiding something, and as they turned the rack, stretching his limbs to the point of agony, his screams grew louder and louder.

He had never touched Catherine after she became Queen! She was no longer interested in him! She cared only for Thomas Culpepper!

And with those words, Catherine's fate was sealed.

Young Thomas Culpepper was one of Henry's favourite companions. Everybody said he was devilishly good-looking, but he had a nasty streak.

A year or so earlier, Culpepper had got away with assaulting a park-keeper's wife and murdering a villager who tried to stop him. People muttered that the King had only pardoned him because he found him so entertaining.

But to a giddy, impressionable young girl, Culpepper was not merely handsome. He was *dangerous* – and to Catherine, that had made him irresistible.

Culpepper was arrested that same day, dragged away from a hunting trip to a cell in the Tower. When he saw the torturers unpacking their instruments, the arrogant smile vanished from his face. Then he, too, began to scream.

Now the truth came out. Catherine had indeed broken off her relationship with Dereham when she became Queen. But a month or two before leaving for the North, she had fallen for Culpepper. She had sent him presents: a cap, a chain, bracelets and a ring.

With incredible foolishness, she had even sent him scribbled love letters, which Henry's men found among Culpepper's belongings. 'It makes my heart die,' she had written, 'to think I cannot be always in your company.'

And there was worse: much worse.

As a courtier, Culpepper had joined the royal party during their journey north. The shadowy stranger outside the Bishop's Palace, that night in Lincoln? That had been Culpepper, waiting for an opportunity to pick the lock and sneak up to Catherine's bedchamber.

It was insanely risky, but Catherine was smitten. She invited him up the next night, too. She sent him a note when the royal party stopped in Pontefract, promising to leave the door open for him. Then she did it again in York.

Just one of these incidents might have been enough to damn her. Taken together, they were a death warrant.

When his men brought Culpepper's confession, Henry sat in silence, his eyes brimming with tears. Never in all his life had he felt so cheated, so humiliated, so betrayed.

On 14 November the terrified Catherine was moved to Syon. Eight days later she was stripped of the title of queen.

Two days after that, she was formally charged with having led 'an abominable, base, carnal, voluptuous and vicious life', and of having tricked and betrayed her master, the King.

As for her old boyfriends, Henry Mannox was released, since he had clearly done nothing wrong. But Francis Dereham and Thomas Culpepper were put on trial, accused of treason.

As always, the verdicts were a foregone conclusion. On 10 December, Dereham was tied to a frame and pulled to Tyburn, where he was hanged, drawn and quartered.

But Culpepper was lucky. Henry still had a trace of affection for his old companion, and Culpepper still had powerful friends. So he had the luxury of a quick death, beneath the executioner's axe.

Catherine spent Christmas at Syon, lonely and miserable. As the days passed, she dared to hope that her husband had forgiven her after all. But this was merely another giddy fantasy.

On 10 February Catherine glanced out of the window, and saw two of Henry's most trusted councillors, the Duke of Suffolk and the Earl of Southampton, with a troop of soldiers. She knew immediately why they had come.

Dressed in black velvet, her face deathly pale, Catherine accompanied them to the riverbank. But when she saw the little covered barge, she panicked and lost her nerve.

'No, no!' she shrieked. She would not go, and they could not make her!

Suffolk nodded at the guards. As Catherine screamed and struggled, they grabbed her by the arms and forced her down into the barge.

A few hours later, the barge glided beneath London Bridge, where the severed heads of Dereham and Culpepper were rotting in the breeze. At the Tower's secret water gate it eased to a halt.

Catherine stumbled out onto the cold stone steps. It was a grey, dreary day, and darkness was falling.

At the top of the steps, the Constable of the Tower bowed his head. He had prepared an apartment for her, he said quietly. He had orders to offer her every comfort, except her freedom.

Catherine was still crying. She had to be helped up to her room. There she threw herself onto her bed, sobbing uncontrollably in terror and desperation.

That night, the Bishop of Lincoln prayed with her for hours. She swore 'in the name of God and his holy angels' that she was innocent and had never betrayed her husband. But it was too late now.

Two nights later, the Constable warned Catherine to prepare herself for execution. He was relieved to see that after the long hours of crying, she had no tears left.

She had a strange last request. She asked if she could see the block on which she was going to be beheaded. Then she spent a few minutes rehearsing, placing her head on it, this way and that.

Monday, 13 February: a chill, cheerless day. Frost glistened on the grass of Tower Green. Mist clung to the steeples of the City.

The guards came for her at seven o'clock.

As they led her up to the scaffold, strewn with straw to mop up the blood, her strength failed her and her knees buckled. The warders had to help her up the last few steps, and even then she could barely stand without assistance.

As she began to speak, in a faint, faltering voice, the

members of Henry's council stood below: black crows, silent and watchful.

Her punishment, she stammered, was 'worthy and just'. She had sinned against God ever since she had been a girl. She deserved a hundred deaths for the way she had treated her husband, and she hoped her listeners would pray for such a generous king.

Catherine stopped speaking. She took off her hood, and turned to kneel. They could see she was absolutely terrified.

She put her head on the block. The executioner lifted his axe, and endless night fell for Catherine Howard.

She was not yet twenty-one years old.

Catherine of Aragon

Anne Boleyn

Jane Seymour

Anne of Cleves

Catherine Howard

Catherine Parr

PART SIX

CATHERINE PARR

18

The Cruel Sea

Two days after Catherine's execution, her former husband returned to London from the countryside.

Henry had been in a black mood for weeks. But now that the axe had fallen, he seemed determined to show the world he was having the time of his life.

For three days he feasted, laughing and joking as if nothing had happened. As always, he paid special attention to the ladies. But would he really take another wife, after everything that had happened?

Henry was now in his early fifties. He had been married five times, and four of his wives were dead.

He was colossally rich, with dozens of palaces, hundreds of paintings, almost two thousand books, thousands of tapestries and countless jewels. All resistance had been crushed. Few people loved him; but everybody feared him.

At the time, artists painted him as a hugely formidable figure, mighty and magnificent. But the reality was very different.

Henry had become enormously fat, with a planet-sized

fifty-four-inch waistline. People muttered that his doublet was so big three men could fit inside it.

Every day he stuffed himself with game pies, stewed sparrows and smoked eels. Haggis, a sheep's stomach stuffed with its minced innards, was another great favourite, washed down with torrents of gin and red wine. And for pudding, he polished off bowl after bowl of custard.

But now he did no exercise to burn it off, not least because he had never recovered from the dreadful jousting accident in the last days of his marriage to Anne Boleyn.

Even now the wound on his left leg had still not healed. Day after day the red-raw ulcer oozed a stinking pus, so foul that his courtiers almost choked at the stench.

Sometimes his leg was so swollen that he stayed in bed for days, his face purple with agony. And sometimes the wound became blocked, the pus building up until his doctors sliced it open, burned it to prevent infection and bandaged it up again.

Not surprisingly, Henry's tournament days were long gone. He was far too sick to hunt. Instead, he preferred to shoot from a stand with bows and muskets, blasting away at deer and birds that his gamekeepers had caught beforehand.

Like many immensely fat people, he struggled to sleep, had to spend hours on the toilet and swallowed countless pills and potions to keep his bowels moving.

To clean out Henry's insides, his doctors would push a greased metal tube up his bottom. The tube was attached to a pig's bladder, and from this the doctors squirted mixtures of salt water and herbs or milk and honey into his bowels.

Naturally enough, all this made him more bad-tempered than ever.

Presented with such a suitor, most sane women would have run a mile. But Henry was not just any fat man in his fifties. He was the King of England.

And in the summer of 1543, the country learned that for the sixth time, he was getting married. This time, the lucky lady's name was Catherine Parr.

What on earth had Catherine Parr done to deserve such a fate? The short answer is – nothing.

At the age of thirty-one, she was a tall, attractive, intelligent woman, with long reddish hair and lively grey eyes. Her father, Sir Thomas, had been a courtier to Henry's father, but had died of the plague when she was just five. In other respects, though, her childhood had been safe and happy.

Her mother, Maud, who had been one of Catherine of Aragon's attendants, made sure that her own Catherine was very well educated. She could read Latin, spoke excellent French, was fascinated by new ideas and loved discussing religion and politics. And not only was she clever, she was kind-hearted and fun. Everybody liked her.

Like many Tudor women, Catherine had grown up

quickly. When she was just seventeen, her mother arranged for her to marry a weedy young man called Sir Edward Burgh. But he died after just four years, leaving her a widow in her early twenties.

By now her mother, too, was dead, which meant Catherine badly needed a new protector. So next she married the rich nobleman Lord Latimer, who was twenty years older.

Although this was far from one of history's great romances, Latimer was a very canny choice. Widowed with two children, he had a fine London townhouse and a magnificent Yorkshire castle. He treated Catherine kindly, and when he died a decade later he left her two manors and plenty of money.

Catherine had played her cards perfectly. She was still young enough to have children, and now she could take her time and pick a husband she really wanted. And she had a particular man in mind: Jane Seymour's dashing brother, Thomas.

At this point, however, Henry barged in. It was more than a year since the execution of Catherine Howard, and many people thought a king was incomplete without a queen.

In any case, Henry was lonely. He needed a wife to help look after his children, especially little Edward, who was almost five. He liked having a pretty woman to talk to in the evenings, and felt awkward sitting alone with the ghosts of his dead brides.

But he knew there could be no repeat of the Howard fiasco. As he told his councillors, he had had 'more than enough of taking young wives', and was determined to find himself a nice, sensible widow.

Catherine Parr was perfect. So that spring, almost out of the blue, Henry asked her to marry him.

For a few days, Catherine hesitated. Her heart belonged to Thomas Seymour, a much younger and more attractive man. It was Thomas's face she saw when she closed her eyes, not Henry's bloated features.

But the King! How could anyone turn down the King?

It was the oldest romantic dilemma of all: love versus duty. Unable to decide, Catherine fell to her knees in prayer, and asked God for help.

Although she was a woman of high passions, she was also deeply religious. For years she had been fascinated by Protestant ideas, and she loved reading and discussing the Bible.

After nights of soul-searching and prayer, she made up her mind. God had given her a chance to help Henry lead England into the new dawn of Protestantism. She could not turn it down.

On 12 July, Henry and Catherine were married in the same room at Hampton Court where he had married Jane Seymour and Anne of Cleves. Their closest friends were on hand to celebrate, though Catherine was too sensible to invite Thomas Seymour.

As the bishop pronounced them husband and wife, a smile spread over Henry's vast features. And at his side, Catherine did her best not to look too disappointed.

As it turned out, though, life as Henry's queen was not really that bad. Elegant palaces, sparkling jewels, lots of money – what was so terrible about that?

Catherine remained as bright and thoughtful as ever, and spent many afternoons with her ladies discussing books and art. But she also loved music and dancing, and had her own troupe of musicians from Venice and Milan. She liked parrots, jesters and flowers, and had a little pet spaniel called Rig, with a velvet collar.

When visitors came to court, she always tried to look her best, wearing her finest gowns and most spectacular diamonds. Many of her gowns had once belonged to Catherine Howard, but in those days nobody thought it odd to wear the last wife's clothes.

Catherine was addicted to shopping. She loved fashion, and was always running up huge bills for gowns in the latest French and Italian styles. And she was obsessed with shoes, buying forty-seven new pairs in a single year.

Visitors always found her an excellent hostess. She was

not greedy or pompous. Even in the snake-pit of Henry's court, almost everybody liked her.

Perhaps the most impressive thing about her, though, was how seriously she took her new role as a stepmother. As her motto she had chosen the phrase 'To be useful in all I do', and she meant every word.

Like Jane Seymour, she made a genuine effort to win over her husband's children. Both Mary and Elizabeth enjoyed her company, and five-year-old Edward took a real shine to her.

Henry, meanwhile, seemed delighted with his new bride. Catherine was a sensible, seasoned woman, not a dizzy teenager, and he knew he could trust her.

After all the years of disappointment and betrayal, he was still an old-fashioned romantic. In one of Catherine's prayer books he scribbled her a little poem:

Remember this writer
when you do pray
for he is yours
none can say nay.

In fact, only one person had a bad word for her. This was Anne of Cleves, who, not surprisingly, had been delighted by the news of Catherine Howard's fall.

Somehow Anne had convinced herself that Henry was bound to come crawling back to her. The news of his marriage to Catherine, therefore, came as a terrible shock. According to the imperial ambassador, Anne almost collapsed in 'great grief and despair'.

After pulling herself together, she pretended that she had never been interested in the King in the first place. 'A fine burden Madam Catherine has taken upon herself!' she declared, adding that Henry was now 'so stout, that such a man has never been seen'.

As for Catherine, Anne announced that Henry's new bride was 'not nearly as beautiful' as she herself was. That was not just unkind but very doubtful, so most people just laughed.

Life at court settled down. The months passed, and soon it was almost a year since Catherine and Henry had been married.

But as their first anniversary approached, black clouds gathered overhead. Across the Channel, the battle drums were beating once again. At Dover, England's fighting men were assembling to take on their oldest and bitterest enemies, the French.

On 11 July 1544, the day before his wedding anniversary, the King's barge pulled away from York Place. Aboard, the ageing Henry gazed out towards the eastern horizon.

He had never lost his love of battle, and had never given up his dreams of glory. Now, for the final time, he was going to war.

War with France had been looming for months. Soon after the execution of Catherine Howard, fighting had broken out between French and imperial armies in Italy. It was only a matter of time before England picked a side.

For Henry, the choice was obvious. Despite his differences with the Emperor, he still dreamed of writing his name in the history books as the man who had conquered France for the English crown.

In his own mind, he was still the dashing young hero who had ridden to victory in so many tournaments, all those years ago. Unfortunately, the reality was rather different.

Henry was now so vast that when his ship reached Calais, he could barely walk down the gangplank. His left leg, with its seeping, reeking ulcer, was so swollen that his magnificent blackened armour had to be cut away.

Merely to get onto his horse, he had to be lifted by a crane and winched up into the saddle, while his men tried very hard not to laugh.

When he walked, he had to use two sticks. He carried a whistle to summon help if he fell over, and spent most of his time shouting at his officers through a primitive megaphone. Needless to say, he was not going to be much use in a fight.

Back at Hampton Court, Catherine waited anxiously for news. As a sign of confidence, Henry had appointed her Queen Regent, with full power while he was gone – just like Catherine of Aragon, all those years ago.

And at first, the reports from France were excellent. By late summer, the English army was camped outside the port of Boulogne. For six weeks they hammered its defences with relentless gunfire. Then, on 11 September, Henry's sappers set off a huge explosion, bringing the walls crashing down.

Two days later, the castle surrendered. As his trumpeters blared out a triumphant fanfare, Henry rode through the shattered walls beneath the flag of St George, 'like a noble and valiant conqueror'.

But fate had a trick up its sleeve. On the very day Henry entered Boulogne in triumph, the Emperor signed a separate peace deal with France. So now the English were left to face the vast French army on their own.

Almost overnight, Henry's hopes of glory had been wiped out. To defend Boulogne and maintain his army across the Channel would be horrendously expensive. What was he going to do?

Another king might have given up. But Henry was nothing if not stubborn. In the next few months, he spent millions of pounds on Boulogne's defences, burning through the remaining money from the old monasteries.

Now the French raised the stakes. In the summer of 1545 a huge fleet set off from the coast of Normandy, heading for England and carrying an invasion force of some 50,000 men.

By 18 July the French had sailed into the Solent, the narrow channel separating the English mainland from the Isle of Wight. From the Hampshire cliffs, children could see the enemy cannons glinting in the haze.

Having returned to England, Henry refused to panic.

As the quays of Portsmouth and Southsea bustled with last-minute preparations, he remained supremely confident.

That night, he dined with his admirals aboard his flagship, the *Great Harry*. Since becoming King, he had spent a fortune on his navy. Nothing could possibly go wrong.

The next morning dawned warm and bright. In the Channel, the sunlight danced on the blue-green waters.

On the battlements of Southsea Castle, a vast figure stood, leaning on a stick, flanked by his courtiers. Henry had come to watch his fleet's glorious victory.

And then – nothing.

The hours went by, and there was no wind. On the English ships, the sails hung limp and loose. The sailors stood anxious and ready; the captains paced the decks impatiently.

In the distance, they could see the French galleys rowing in to attack their outlying barges. But without a breeze, the heavy English warships were unable to move, and could only watch in helpless frustration.

Midday came and went. In the distance, the sun slowly began to dip. At Southsea, Henry stood grim-faced. None of his courtiers dared to speak.

And then, after hours of waiting, there came a breath of air. The sails stirred; the flags fluttered. Roars of joy echoed across Portsmouth Harbour.

The *Great Harry* was moving at last, a glorious spectacle in the late afternoon sun. And close by, picking up speed, was Henry's favourite ship, the splendid *Mary Rose*, with her towering castles and gleaming guns.

Although the *Mary Rose* had been launched more than thirty years earlier, she remained a magnificent sight, bursting with soldiers and bristling with cannons. In her way, she was a little outpost of England, packed with at least 400 gunners and archers, cooks and carpenters, sailors and surgeons.

Now the waiting was over. The pipes and flutes had been put away, the dice and backgammon forgotten. And as the sails of the *Mary Rose* swelled with the breeze, the sailors' hearts filled with patriotic pride.

Here was the perfect war machine. Every part worked in harmony with the next, as if she were some huge clockwork model in wood and brass.

Cannon fire echoed across the harbour. There was the sound of screaming and splintering now, as the English flagships poured death and destruction into the French galleys. On the battlements, the corners of Henry's mouth twitched in a smile of satisfaction.

Fire and thunder burst from the *Mary Rose*'s starboard guns. Cheers rose from the men on deck. The ship was turning now, preparing to fire from the other side. A sudden gust of wind ruffled the waters of the harbour.

And then, as if in slow motion, Henry's beloved ship seemed to falter in mid-turn. Beside him on the battlements, somebody gasped in horror. The King's eyes widened, the smile frozen on his lips.

Something had gone horribly wrong. The *Mary Rose* was leaning too far to starboard. Surely she would right herself? But no – she was lurching, tipping, falling . . .

On deck, the cheers of joy had become screams of

panic. As the ship toppled, the equipment below decks was coming loose: the colossal oven, the copper cauldron, even the heavy guns. Men were shrieking and scrambling in terror. The decks were crowded with contorted bodies.

Since few of the ship's crew could swim, they knew that if she capsized, they were dead. But everything was happening so fast. One moment the *Mary Rose* was turning. The next, with a terrible sound of snapping and shattering, she was down.

For a moment or two, the spectators on the shore could see hundreds of little figures flailing desperately in the foaming waters. At this distance, they seemed so tiny, so vulnerable, clinging vainly to the timbers as the ship disappeared beneath the waves. The screams grew fainter and fainter. And then there was only silence.

On the battlements Henry just stood there, frozen with shock. 'Oh, my gentlemen!' he said brokenly. 'Oh, my gallant men!'

Then, at last, he turned away.

The loss of the *Mary Rose* was one of the greatest disasters in English naval history. Yet nobody ever discovered why it had happened. Even when the ship was finally recovered from the deep, more than four centuries later, the mystery remained.

But Henry was lucky. The wind died down, and his fleet managed to regroup and fight off the attackers. By nightfall the Battle of the Solent had petered out into a draw, and after a few days the enemy fleet retreated to France.

Eventually, and very reluctantly, Henry signed a peace treaty. He could keep Boulogne for eight years, but then he had to give it back.

So, after wasting millions of pounds and thousands of lives, he had nothing to show for it. There would be no English empire in France, and he would never be remembered as one of history's great military commanders.

Henry would never fight another war. He was old and tired, and his dreams of glory lay in ruins.

He was very close to the end now. But there would be more tears, and even more bloodshed, before it was over.

19

The King Is Dead

It was the spring of 1546, and dusk was falling at the palace of Whitehall. Behind the windows of the Queen's apartments, candlelight flickered on the faces in the circle.

Catherine and her ladies-in-waiting were reading the Bible. Beside her sat one of her chaplains, who occasionally murmured a few words of explanation or encouragement.

Catherine's Bible meetings had become a daily ritual. Every afternoon she and her friends met to read the holy book in English, their heads bowed in respectful prayer.

Meanwhile, in a distant corner of the maze, a huge, hulking figure brooded alone in the shadowed gloom of his study.

Henry felt old now, old and sick and weary. So many of his old companions were dead. Wolsey was dead, and More was dead, and Cromwell was dead . . .

Sometimes, infuriated with his councillors, Henry snarled that he missed Cromwell, the best adviser he had ever had. And then he remembered what had happened to him, and his voice tailed away.

Of course, he was lucky to have Catherine, but the ghosts of his vanished brides never left him in peace. There was Catherine Howard, the traitor. There was poor Jane, whom God had taken from him.

There was Anne, with her black eyes and sharp tongue . . . Anne, for whom he had sacrificed so much . . .

And then there was the first Catherine, who had fought him for so long. He could still remember meeting her before Arthur's wedding, when he was a boy. A little Spanish girl with long fair hair . . .

They had been so young. It all seemed such a long time ago . . .

All the time Henry felt tired. He was so fat, and his legs were so swollen, that he had to be carried around on velvet-lined chairs. His ulcers caused him terrible pain, and he seemed unable to shake off colds and fevers.

He lay awake at night, unable to sleep. At Catherine's suggestion he had started wearing glasses to read, because his eyesight was so bad.

One day, leafing through a magnificent illustrated Bible, he came across Psalm 37, which contains the line: 'I have been young, and now am old.'

In the margin, Henry scribbled in Latin: 'A painful saying.'

Outside the study door, in the darkness of the labyrinth, the King's councillors whispered and waited.

The court was more bitterly divided than ever. The great noble families still looked to the ageing, cold-hearted Duke of Norfolk, the supreme survivor, who had clung to his position despite Catherine Howard's disgrace.

Norfolk and his sneering son, Henry, Earl of Surrey, saw themselves as the champions of the old order. When the King was dead, they planned to seize control of little Prince Edward and lead England back to Rome.

Against them stood the 'new men', who had worked their way up the ladder and were often keen Protestants. Their leader was the little prince's uncle, Edward Seymour, Jane Seymour's eldest brother.

When his sister married the King, Seymour had been made Earl of Hertford. A keen Protestant, he had been one of Henry's chief commanders during the war against the French.

Hertford was a man of burning, hard-nosed ambition. He was determined that when Henry died, he, not Norfolk, would take charge of the boy prince. But he knew he must strike quickly, for there could only be one winner.

As the wolf packs circled, their fangs bared, Henry knew precisely what was happening. It was all part of his plan. He was still safeguarding his position as their ringmaster.

Secretive, bitter and lonely, the old King trusted no one. His spies were everywhere, listening in the shadows.

Over every meeting, every banquet, every look, every smile, hung an atmosphere of dread. One moment you were Henry's favourite, rewarded with wealth and honours. The next, the Captain of the Guard was leading you into an execution cell at the Tower of London.

Norfolk's son, the Earl of Surrey, was a vain, snobbish hooligan. But he was also an excellent poet, and in one of his verses he perfectly captured the mood at court:

> *I saw a royal throne, whereas that Justice should have sit;*
> *Instead of whom I saw, with fierce and cruel mood,*
> *Where Wrong was sat, that bloody beast, that drunk the*
> *   guiltless blood.*

It is pretty obvious whom Surrey meant by the 'bloody beast'. He meant Henry.

In the Queen's chamber, the Bible meeting was over. As her ladies put away their prayer books, Catherine asked her chaplain for a private word.

As Queen, she had worked unceasingly to promote Protestant ideas. She was convinced that the route to heaven lay not in following priests and popes, but in reading the Bible and finding God's 'grace and goodness' within yourself. She had even published her own prayer book, handing out copies to friends and allies.

But now, Catherine said quietly, she was frightened. She knew Norfolk and Surrey would stop at nothing to secure power. And she knew that by taking sides in the deadly dispute between Protestants and Catholics, she had made herself a target.

Ever since the death of Cromwell, six years earlier, the pendulum had swung back and forth. One moment Henry seemed to favour the forces of change; the next, he leaned back towards the old ways.

He had broken with Rome and destroyed the monasteries, but he kept the title Defender of the Faith and burned Protestants who went too far.

He mocked pilgrimages and relics, but he still believed in the magic of the Mass. And although he had ordered an English Bible to be used in churches across the kingdom, he banned most women, apprentices and the poor from reading it.

Every day, the King seemed to change his mind. No wonder ordinary people did not know what to believe. They did not even know what they were *supposed* to believe.

Now, in the early months of 1546, Catherine could feel the mood changing. Henry seemed more impatient, more unpredictable than ever. All the time, Norfolk and his allies were whispering in the darkness, pouring poison in his ear, urging him to crack down on the Protestants.

Already Catherine had bought new strongboxes for her chambers, with new locks to deter prying eyes. She hid some of her religious books in her toilet, and persuaded her friends to smuggle others out of the palace.

But every day, she could feel the old guard staring at her, their eyes hard with hatred. She could feel the net closing around her, as it had closed around Anne Boleyn and Catherine Howard.

Summer approached. The heat rose. In the palace, the tension felt almost suffocating now.

On 24 May, Norfolk's allies arrested a young woman from Lincolnshire called Anne Askew. She had court connections: her brother had a junior post in the royal household.

More importantly, Anne was a fervent Protestant who believed all men and women had the right to read the Bible. She was the tool the old guard would use to bring down the Queen.

Locked in the Tower of London, Askew was questioned again and again about her supposed connections with Catherine's ladies-in-waiting. When she denied it, Norfolk's friends tied her to a rack and turned the cranks, stretching her body until the bones popped from their sockets.

But Anne said nothing. She would never betray the Queen. She did not even cry out, but merely bit her lip while the tears ran down her agonized face.

Catherine was safe – or so it seemed. But then, only a couple of weeks later, she made a terrible mistake.

One evening she and Henry were discussing religion with the Bishop of Winchester, and for a moment she forgot herself. Before she knew what she was doing, she was interrupting her husband, her voice rising with passion as she lectured him about the true path to heaven.

Then she saw the expression on Henry's face, and stopped. It was too late. The damage was done.

The bishop could see how furious he was. And by a terrible mischance, the bishop was one of Norfolk's closest allies.

In the next few weeks, Catherine's enemies sharpened their knives for the kill. By early July their plans were ready.

The Queen would be arrested by the Captain of the Guard and taken by barge to the Tower. Her rooms would be searched for dangerous or illegal books, and her ladies would be arrested and broken under torture.

She would be charged with heresy and treason. There was only one possible outcome. Death.

And then, quite suddenly, the wheel of fortune took an unexpected turn.

In the last few months, Henry's legs had become so painful that they required regular care. As the doctors changed his bandages, the King liked to talk. One evening, he mentioned to one of his favourite doctors, Thomas Wendy, that he was losing patience with the Queen.

At once Wendy's ears pricked up. He, too, was a keen Protestant, and the last thing he wanted was to see Catherine in trouble.

What happened next was very mysterious. The following day, one of Catherine's ladies noticed a piece of paper in the corridor outside her apartments. When she opened it, her eyes widened in horror.

It was a version of the charges against her mistress – the charges that would surely result in death.

When Catherine read the note herself, she almost collapsed in shock. But as she lay on her bed, choking back tears of terror, she saw a familiar face in the doorway. It was Doctor Wendy.

All was not lost, he whispered. If she went to her husband at once, and threw herself on his mercy, she might be able to save herself.

A lesser woman might have buckled. But in this desperate hour, when she knew the wrong word could seal her fate, Catherine found her courage.

A few moments later, adopting her most obedient expression, she swept down the corridor towards the King's chamber.

Henry glanced up, his face cold. Had she come to lecture him about religion?

Not at all, Catherine said meekly. She was a mere woman, and he was her master. She wanted only to learn from a 'prince of such excellent learning and wisdom . . . my only anchor, Supreme Head and Governor here on earth, next unto God'.

Henry frowned. This was not what he had expected. Hadn't she set herself up as the great expert, telling him what he should believe?

Catherine smiled. She knew she had 'meddled', she said. But she had only done it to distract her beloved husband from the pain in his legs – and to learn from his great wisdom.

It was a lie, of course. But it was perfect. It was exactly what Henry wanted to hear.

'Is it even so, sweetheart?' he said, and smiled. 'Then perfect friends we are now again.' And he held out his arms.

Inwardly, Catherine breathed an enormous sigh of relief. She was safe.

Yet, just a few days later, there was a grim reminder of what might have awaited her, if she and Dr Wendy had not acted so quickly.

On 16 July, poor Anne Askew was taken to the market at Smithfield, to be burned as a heretic. Her body had been so broken by torture that she could not walk or stand unaided. She lay slumped in a chair, which her guards tied to the stake.

It was a stifling day. A storm was brewing, and the crowd was restless. One or two men shouted that Anne was a good Christian; others rounded on them, and scuffles broke out.

Suddenly a great clap of thunder tore the sky in two – the voice of God, some people cried. And as if in answer, the bonfire burst into an explosion of its own.

When the smoke cleared, it was obvious what had happened. Somebody had hidden gunpowder under the wood, so that Anne's suffering would not be prolonged.

It was another sign that, in the dark heart of Henry's kingdom, nothing was ever quite as it seemed.

Autumn came. The King was weaker than ever now, and it was obvious he did not have long left. At court, the tension was stretched to breaking point.

By now Norfolk and Hertford no longer bothered to hide their loathing. Their spies were said to be at work across the country, collecting information before the inevitable bloodbath. No one could be trusted. No conversation was safe.

Norfolk's plan was simple. As soon as Henry was dead, he would seize Prince Edward, install himself as regent and hand power to the old nobility.

The key figure was his son, the Earl of Surrey. Boastful, dashing and dandyish, Surrey was popular with the London crowds. When the time came, he would take the lead in crushing the Protestant upstarts.

But as Norfolk put the finishing touches to his plan, Hertford was whispering in the King's ear. Unless they struck now, he murmured, there would be nobody to protect Prince Edward. Norfolk and Surrey had set their sights on the crown, and the Tudor dynasty would be destroyed.

As the nights drew in, Henry brooded alone. And at last he made up his mind.

On the afternoon of 2 December, Surrey strolled into the Great Hall with the swagger of a man who knew power was only weeks away. Waiting for him was the Captain of the Guard, who had a favour to ask. He needed help with a private matter; could he have a quiet word?

Surrey nodded. The captain ushered him into a quiet corridor. And as Surrey took in the twelve hard-faced soldiers waiting in the shadows, his jaw dropped with horrified realization.

It all happened so quickly that he had no time to think. One moment he was sauntering through the Great Hall; the next he was shivering on a barge, bound for the Tower.

Norfolk was in the country when he heard of his son's arrest. Just as his enemies expected, he rode immediately to the palace, and once again the guards were waiting. By nightfall, he, too, was in the Tower, hammering desperately on the door, screaming for the King.

At Whitehall, the candles burned long into the night. Hertford's agents were busy preparing the list of treason charges.

In just a few hours, everything had changed. The doors to the King's apartments were closed. Only Hertford and his men were allowed in and out.

Inside, Henry sat propped up in bed, his breathing hoarse and laboured, his spectacles perched on the end of his nose. He was reading the list of charges.

Occasionally his eyes narrowed and he scribbled something in the margin.

At last he glanced up and met Hertford's eye. Slowly, coldly, Henry nodded.

The struggle was over. The Protestants had won.

On Christmas Eve, Catherine took a barge down to Greenwich. She knew her husband was dying, and she had no desire to spend Christmas in an atmosphere of terror.

With her, she brought Mary and Elizabeth. For a few days, at least, the three of them were able to forget the plotting and enjoy the festive celebrations.

In the Tower, Norfolk was pleading for his life. Again and again he sent tear-stained letters to the King's bedside. But no reply ever came.

Frantic with terror, Norfolk agreed to sign a confession, prepared by his captors. He had, he admitted, kept 'secret the false acts of my son . . . I confess my crime no less than high treason and although I do not deserve it, humbly beg his Highness to have pity on me'.

With that, his son's fate was sealed.

The very next day, Surrey was condemned to death. As

Hertford's voice echoed around the court, his victim could not restrain himself.

'Of what have you found me guilty?' he spat angrily. 'I know the King wants to get rid of the noble blood around him, and to employ none but low people!'

But it did him no good. On 19 January, the guards led Surrey out onto Tower Hill. There, shivering in the cold winter air, Henry's last victim met his end.

Henry was now very ill indeed, his chest rising and falling with a painful effort, his face deathly grey. Confined to bed, he drifted in and out of sleep.

Around him, Hertford and his allies were preparing for the future. As Henry slept, they fixed his stamp to document after document, granting themselves ever more lands, riches and titles. Their master was dying, and they were feasting like vultures on the spoils.

It was a bleak, freezing January. On the windows of Wolsey's old palace, the rain battered relentlessly down.

By the morning of Thursday, 27 January, Henry was fading fast. In the darkened corners of the palace, the courtiers huddled in little groups.

Not long before noon, the King's friend Sir Anthony Denny knelt by the splendidly carved walnut bed. The doctors were agreed, he murmured. There were only hours left now. Henry should prepare for the end, and remember his sins like a 'good Christian man'.

A desperate rasping sound came from the great figure on the bed. The 'mercy of Christ', Henry whispered, would surely 'pardon me all my sins, yea, though they were greater than can be'.

Denny asked if he wanted to see a priest. Henry gave a painful nod. 'It should be Dr Cranmer,' he mumbled, 'but I will first take a little sleep and then, as I feel myself, I will advise upon the matter.'

They were the last words he ever said. Moments later, his head fell back onto the pillow.

Travelling slowly on the frozen roads, Archbishop Cranmer did not arrive until just after midnight. He found the palace dark and silent. Henry was still breathing, but he had barely stirred for hours.

Climbing onto the huge bed, Cranmer took Henry's hand and urged him to show, one last time, that he loved Jesus Christ and 'trusted in the Lord'.

Henry said nothing. All that could be heard was the terrible, laboured wheezing.

Then Cranmer felt the huge hand squeeze his own. He nodded at the men waiting in the gloom. The King, he felt sure, was ending his days in the love of Christ.

Still they waited. The dying man's breathing became fainter, and fainter . . . and then at last it stopped.

Henry was dead. It was finished.

The Tomb

For a moment, nobody moved in the darkened bedchamber. There was a long, appalled silence, as if none of them could really believe Henry had gone.

Cranmer stood and bowed his head. The Earl of Hertford did the same. One by one, Henry's councillors stepped forward to pay their respects to their departed master, his body stiffening and silent on the huge wooden bed.

Hertford's mind was on the future. He had been preparing for this moment for weeks. Now it was time to put his plan into operation.

The doors of Henry's apartments remained firmly closed, and his meals were still delivered as usual. Nothing had changed. There must be no whisper of the King's death until everything was ready.

In secret, orders went out immediately to the ports. By morning, England was sealed off, while Hertford's troops took control of the main roads around London. Nobody could come in or out without his permission.

A few hours later, Hertford rode north with 300 soldiers. Soon after midnight on Saturday, 29 January, he arrived outside the castle, twenty-five miles from London, where his nephew, the nine-year-old Prince Edward, was sleeping.

When his men had woken the prince, Hertford turned south with him to Enfield, where Princess Elizabeth was staying. Only then did he break the news to the two children. Their father was dead – and Edward was King.

Two days later the Lord Chancellor announced Henry's death to Parliament. The news travelled fast. In every village in the country, the church bells tolled in mourning.

As crowds gathered for special services, there was no rejoicing. Most people were shocked and frightened, and many were in floods of tears.

Henry might have been a monster. But he had been *their* monster, a great and formidable man. After a thirty-eight-year reign, most men and women could remember no other king. What would happen to England now?

The answer came within hours. That afternoon, the young Edward VI rode through the streets of the City, surrounded by Hertford's soldiers. Cheers rose on every side. Trumpets blared from the walls of the Tower. Cannons blasted from the barges on the Thames.

Hertford's plan had worked perfectly. His nephew's crown was secured, while he himself became Duke of Somerset and Lord Protector of the Realm. The wheel had turned, and the Seymour family stood supreme.

But even amid the cheers and the cannon fire,

there were the faint sounds of whispers in the shadows. The King was dead, but the game went on.

At the palace of Whitehall, the servants were cleaning Henry's body for burial.

They pulled out his entrails and washed the vast corpse with wine, before dressing it with sweet-scented spices to mask the smell of decay. Cleaned, purged and perfumed, it was wrapped in a huge waxed cloth, before being wrapped again in velvet and tied up with silk.

Next, Henry's embalmed body was lifted into a huge lead shell, which was then lifted into a gigantic coffin of solid elm. A golden cloth was draped over the coffin, with a cross on the top. As candles flickered in the gloom, Henry's chaplains kept watch, their heads bent in prayer.

Five days later, the servants moved the coffin into the great golden chariot that would carry it to Windsor. As the bells tolled again, the chariot rolled through the streets behind a long procession of priests and soldiers.

On 16 February, the Yeomen of the Guard lowered Henry's coffin into the vault at St George's Chapel, Windsor. There he would rest for all eternity, alongside his third wife, Jane Seymour.

When it was done, the Lord Protector stepped forward and broke his white staff of office in two. Then he threw the pieces into the vault, to show that the days of the old king were over.

A voice cried: 'Long live King Edward!', and they all took up the cry. Then the trumpets sounded one last time, and it was done.

Catherine Parr watched the funeral from a window overlooking the choir, dressed in dark velvet. Like everybody else, she bowed her head in prayer as Henry's body was lowered into the vault.

She was not sorry to have become a widow again. Freed from the terror of Henry's court, she was still the first lady in England. And in his will her husband had left her a fortune in jewels, coins and lands.

Catherine wasted no time in starting again. A few months later, she secretly married the man she had always really wanted: the Lord Protector's younger brother, Thomas Seymour.

A handsome, roguish fellow, Seymour moved in with Catherine at the Old Manor, Chelsea, on the banks of the Thames. There they lived with her teenage stepdaughter,

Elizabeth, and Lady Jane Grey, Elizabeth's cousin. And for a time, life seemed perfect.

But after the first year, something went wrong. Elizabeth was fourteen now, red-haired and striking. And one morning, Catherine came into her stepdaughter's bedroom and caught Thomas trying to kiss her.

So that was the end of that. Although she loved Elizabeth dearly, the girl had to go.

Then came some good news. Catherine was expecting a baby. She moved to the country to prepare for the great event, and on 30 August she gave birth to a little girl, called Mary.

But now, when she needed it most, Catherine's luck deserted her. Like Jane Seymour, she fell ill with a fever.

For six days she fought for life, but in the early hours of 5 September 1548, she died. She had survived Henry by less than two years.

For Henry's three children, too, fortune's wheel continued to turn.

Edward VI was the best-educated king England had ever had. Taught by scholars from the universities of Oxford and Cambridge, he learned Latin, French, Spanish and Italian. He studied maths, geography and astronomy, learned to play the lute and collected globes and maps.

Above all, this pale, slight, fair-haired boy was intensely religious. A passionate Protestant, he read long sections of the Bible every day. And as he entered his teens, he saw himself as the champion of the true faith, chosen by God to lead his people into the light.

Under Edward and his uncle, the Lord Protector, England was engulfed in a tide of revolution. Most of the old Catholic rituals, traditions and feast days were banned. So were religious processions and plays, as well as candles and shrines in churches.

The traditional maypoles, around which villagers danced on May Day, were chopped down. And, most shockingly of all, all images in churches were forbidden.

In every corner of England, saints' pictures were torn down, stained-glass windows shattered, wooden crosses burned, painted walls covered with whitewash. In some churches even the altars were smashed, as the Protestants sought to destroy all traces of the old order.

Once again, England reeled under the shock of the new. In the summer of 1549 a wave of rebellions swept across the countryside, and thousands of people were killed.

At court, many people blamed the arrogance of the Lord Protector. Eventually his fellow councillors turned against him and, like so many ambitious men before him, the Duke of Somerset was arrested, dragged to the Tower and beheaded.

The Protestant revolution went on, but there was a cloud on the horizon. In the spring of 1552 Edward fell ill with measles, and he never really recovered. A year later, a heavy cold turned into a serious lung disease, and by the early summer it was obvious he was dying.

Edward died on the evening of 6 July 1553. Even in his last words, he thought only of his Protestant mission. 'O Lord God, save thy chosen people of England!' he gasped. 'O my Lord God, defend this realm from Papistry, and maintain thy true religion!'

He was still only fifteen years old.

So Henry's worst nightmare had come true. After a reign lasting barely six years, his son had died young, and there was no male Tudor to succeed him.

The crown ought to have passed to Catherine of Aragon's daughter Mary. But Mary was a committed Catholic, and Edward was desperate to stop his sister from reversing his religious revolution.

As he lay dying, he named his Protestant cousin Lady Jane Grey, another teenager, as his successor. Poor Jane was horrified when she heard the news, and immediately burst into tears. But the Protestant lords were determined to use her as their instrument, and there was not much she could do about it.

Jane Grey's reign did not last long either, though.

Mary had been waiting for this moment all her life. After just nine days, she rode to London at the head of an army. Poor Jane was arrested, sent to the Tower and eventually beheaded.

Now, thirty-seven-year-old Mary ruled as Queen of England. Hoping to have children of her own, she married the Emperor Charles's eldest son, Philip of Spain. But Philip spent little time in England, and no child ever came.

Mary had not changed. As solemn and serious as ever, she was determined to turn back the clock and restore her mother's Catholic faith.

In the five years of her reign almost 300 Protestants were burned at the stake, from ordinary men and women to great and learned bishops. Even her father's old friend, the kindly, scholarly Thomas Cranmer, was not safe.

Arrested and charged with heresy, the old Archbishop claimed to have changed his mind, and said he had returned to the Catholic faith. But then he rediscovered his courage, and told a crowd in Oxford that he had only 'confessed' because he had been afraid of death.

When he was burned, Cranmer said, he would put his right hand into the flames first, because it had written the false confession. 'And as for the Pope,' he cried, 'I refuse him, as Christ's enemy and Antichrist!'

Cranmer was executed later that day. At the stake he showed extraordinary calm and courage. 'I see the heavens open,' he cried out at the end, 'and Jesus standing at the right hand of God!'

In London, Mary seethed with fury. She had been so sure that the ordinary people of England were desperate to return to their Catholic faith. Yet even as these heretics burned, they were winning the battle for hearts and minds.

In truth, Mary was simply too late. England was a very young country, and about half the population were children or teenagers.

By the time she became Queen, many could not even remember the days of shrines and relics. They had been brought up to hate and fear the Pope, not to follow him.

The Catholic England of miracles and monasteries, the England that had welcomed Mary's mother as a girl, was gone. It would never return.

Only one of Henry's brides was still alive now.

Almost twenty years after she had made the crossing to England, Anne of Cleves was in her early forties. She cut a slightly gloomy, matronly figure, always complaining about how expensive everything in England was.

For a long time she hoped to return home to Germany. 'I might come to life again among my friends,' she wrote grumpily, although she feared they had 'forgotten all about me by now'.

But nobody was prepared to lend her money for the trip. Even her brother, now Duke of Cleves, was not very keen to see her, because he only sent her enough cash to pay off some of her debts.

So Anne remained at court. As the wheel turned, she looked on in baffled disbelief, shaking her head at the strange passions of the English.

'God knows what will happen next!' she wrote to her brother after the death of the Duke of Somerset. And then, entirely typically, she returned to her favourite subject. 'Everything is so costly in this country . . .'

At last, in the summer of 1557, the great survivor fell ill. On 16 July, at Catherine Parr's old house in Chelsea, she died.

Anne was buried in Westminster Abbey with all the pomp and ceremony befitting a queen of England. There was a grand procession, with all the mourners dressed in black, just as she would have wanted.

But even in death, fate was against her. London was experiencing a summer heat wave, and the authorities urged people to stay at home and keep cool instead of coming to the abbey.

As a result, there were no crowds to mourn her passing. But poor Anne of Cleves had never enjoyed much luck in England, so she would probably not have been surprised.

After months of ill health, Mary died on 17 November 1558, aged forty-two. Much of her life had been a long, sad struggle against formidable odds.

But there was no happy ending. For centuries afterwards, people remembered her as 'Bloody Mary', the woman who had burned the Protestant martyrs.

Now the crown passed to her Protestant half-sister Elizabeth, the daughter of Anne Boleyn. At the age of twenty-five, Elizabeth, too, had endured plenty of fear and heartache.

But she had watched her father, brother and sister closely, and had learned the art of survival. Her spymasters had agents everywhere, watching for traitors. And she always moved carefully, cautiously, anxious not to provoke another rebellion.

Reversing Mary's changes, Elizabeth broke with Rome and restored the Church of England, with herself as Supreme Governor. But her new Church of England was deliberately broad, with a mixture of Protestant ideas and Catholic traditions, to appeal to as many people as possible.

The years went by. In London, a young man called William Shakespeare began to make his name as an actor and playwright. Abroad, sea captains such as Sir Francis Drake and Sir John Hawkins won wealth and fame against the great treasure-fleets of Spain.

Enraged, the Spanish sent a mighty armada to invade England, overthrow Elizabeth and restore Catholic rule. But in the summer of 1588, Drake and his fellow captains won a glorious victory, and the Queen's reputation as a national heroine was assured.

There was a personal price for Elizabeth's survival, though. She had seen the tears and turmoil of her father's marriages, and was determined not to fall into the same trap.

So she became the Virgin Queen, married only to her country. For almost half a century she ruled alone, dedicated to 'all my husbands, my good people'.

On 24 March 1603, at the age of sixty-nine, Elizabeth died peacefully in her bed.

She had ruled for longer than her brother and sister combined, and longer than either her father or grandfather. But she had no heir, so the crown passed to her closest Protestant relative, King James VI of Scotland.

Anne Boleyn's daughter had been the last of the Tudors. When she was gone, the dynasty passed into history.

Elizabeth died almost exactly 101 years after another Tudor, her father's brother Arthur, was struck down by sweating sickness at Ludlow Castle.

If Arthur had lived, and had gone on to have children with Catherine of Aragon, the course of history would have been very different.

Henry VIII would never have become king. Mary, Elizabeth and Edward would never have been born.

Anne Boleyn, Jane Seymour, Catherine Howard and Catherine Parr would probably have married English noblemen. And Anne of Cleves might have lived out her days in Germany, happily married to some local duke.

Even after Arthur died, history did not *have* to work out the way it did. If any of Catherine's baby sons had lived, or if Mary had been a boy, Henry would probably never have wanted a divorce.

In that case, England might never have broken with Rome. Its people would have seen themselves as part of the wide Catholic family, Europeans like any other. Instead, they came to think of themselves as a nation apart, chosen by God to fight for freedom.

Today people still have their favourites among the six wives of Henry VIII. Waspish Anne Boleyn, or gentle Jane Seymour? The bewildered, much-mocked Anne of Cleves? Giddy, reckless Catherine Howard, or steady, sensible Catherine Parr?

And then there is Henry himself. Was he a mischievous, fun-loving little boy, or a fat, greedy, brooding invalid? A sportsman, an art lover, a bully or a braggart? A strong ruler who stood up for England, or a selfish tyrant who tore it apart?

The answer, of course, is that he was all of them.

But perhaps the most moving character of all was the girl who sailed to England as a nervous teenager, sent to marry a young man she had never seen, who spoke a language she could not understand, and found herself plunged into a terrifying world of secrets and lies.

As a girl, Catherine of Aragon had dreamed of the romantic world of King Arthur's court. Her own life turned out very differently, and she tasted more than her share of heartbreak and humiliation.

But the girl from Castile never, ever gave up. And even as she lay dying, betrayed by her husband and cut off from her daughter, she prayed for Henry, not for herself.

Today Catherine's tomb lies in Peterborough Cathedral. Every year, on the anniversary of her burial, there is a special service in her memory.

The inscription around the tombstone reads: 'A Queen Cherished By the English People For Her Loyalty, Piety, Courage and Compassion'.

And when you visit her tomb, there are almost always fresh flowers.

AUTHOR'S NOTE

Catherine's tomb at Peterborough is not the only Tudor site you can visit today.

At Bosworth you can trace the footsteps of the knights who fought for Richard III and Henry Tudor. In Granada, you can follow Catherine's ghost through the gardens of the Alhambra. At Hampton Court Palace you can see the cavernous kitchens where Henry VIII's cooks sweated to produce his banquets. At Portsmouth Dockyard you can visit the wreck of the *Mary Rose*, dragged up from its watery grave. And at the Tower of London you can see the infamous Traitors' Gate, where Henry's victims were brought by barge on their way to their deaths.

Countless books have been written about the six wives of Henry VIII, and probably nobody has ever read all of them. But I did read the excellent books by Antonia Fraser, Alison Weir and David Starkey, and learned an enormous amount from all three. And I am hugely indebted to historians such as Eric Ives, David Loades, J. J. Scarisbrick, Retha Warnicke, John Guy, Susan Brigden, Peter Marshall, Diarmaid MacCulloch, Tracy Borman, Giles Tremlett and Robert Hutchinson, whose books I raided for anecdotes and insights.

Once again, thank you to Simon Winder, Eva Hodgkin

and James Pullen for reading with such care, and to every-body at the Wylie Agency, Penguin and Particular Books. Thank you to Julia Bruce for going through it so tolerantly. A special thank you, as always, to Catherine for all your love and encouragement.

Above all, thank you to Arthur, who read each chapter as I wrote it, solemnly ticking every battle, every massacre and every severed head, and giving me extra points for hangings, drawings and quarterings. I could not have asked for a more enthusiastic – or more bloodthirsty – reader.